I0154837

Facing the Future with Hope

*Cycle B Sermons for Advent,
Christmas, and Epiphany
Based on the Gospel Texts*

Richard A. Hasler

CSS Publishing Company, Inc.
Lima, Ohio

FIRST EDITION
Copyright © 2011
by CSS Publishing Co., Inc.

Published by CSS Publishing Company, Inc., Lima, Ohio 45807. All rights reserved. No part of this publication may be reproduced in any manner whatsoever without the prior permission of the publisher, except in the case of brief quotations embodied in critical articles and reviews. Inquiries should be addressed to: CSS Publishing Company, Inc., Permissions Department, 5450 N. Dixie Highway, Lima, Ohio 45807.

Scripture quotations are from the New Revised Standard Version of the Bible. Copyright 1989 by the Division of Christian Education of the National Council of the Churches of Christ in the USA. Used by permission.

Library of Congress Cataloging-in-Publication Data

Hasler, Richard A.
    Facing the future with hope : sermons for Advent, Christmas, and Epiphany : Cycle B Gospel texts / Richard A. Hasler. -- 1st ed.
        p. cm.
    ISBN 0-7880-2644-5 (alk. paper)
    1. Bible. N.T. Gospels--Sermons. 2. Church year sermons. 3. Sermons, American--21st century. 4. Common lectionary (1992). Year B. I. Title.

    BS2555.54.H37 2011
    252'.6--dc22   2011013506

For more information about CSS Publishing Company resources, visit our website at www.csspub.com or email us at csr@csspub.com or call (800) 241-4056.

ISBN-13: 978-0-7880-2644-7
ISBN-10: 0-7880-2644-5
PRINTED IN USA

For our children and their spouses: Karen Kelly and her husband Mike Kelly and Rick Hasler and his wife Cindy Hasler and also for our grandchildren: Michael Kelly, Katie Kelly, Erin Kelly, Jennifer Hasler, and Lindsay Hasler. These are my "geeks" who are always ready to rescue me when I have computer problems.

Table of Contents

Introduction

I often listen to the choir of St. Olaf College in Minnesota on the radio or watch them on television. One time during intermission the announcer asked one of the choir members why she took obvious delight in singing in the choir. She replied, "When I sing I become part of a song that began long before I arrived here and will continue long after I am gone."[1]

When we sing our hymns and our favorite Christmas carols we indeed become part of a song that began long before we arrived here and will continue long after we have gone. As we begin the cycle of the Christian year in our worship once again, we connect our small personal stories with the larger story of Jesus — his birth, life, teachings, sufferings, death, and resurrection. When we link our individual lives with his grand story we gain meaning and purpose. We realize we are going somewhere. We have a compass that gives us direction.

The Christian year begins with the season of Advent and closes with the long season of the Sundays after Pentecost, sometimes referred to as "Ordinary Time." Following the year through the cycle of its major festivals and changing seasons gives balance, breadth, and direction for preaching and worship leadership.

These particular sermons focus on Advent, Christmas, and Epiphany. Advent, the first season, the four Sundays prior to Christmas, sounds the note of anticipation and expectancy as we approach Christmas. If we ask ourselves as individuals or as a congregation, "Do we have a future?" Advent answers unmistakably in the affirmative.

Christmas is both a day and a season. We frequently ask ourselves the question, "When is the right time?" Should we act now or wait longer? Christmas reminds us that Jesus was born at the right time, "in the fullness of time." Therefore, Christmas suggests we too can expect *kairos* moments, creative breakthroughs, when God brings forth birth and rebirth in our own lives.

Epiphany begins on January 6, once again a day and a season extending to the beginning of Lent. As a congregation we periodically ask, "How inclusive should we be?" Epiphany symbolizes the universality of the gospel. The coming of the wise men from outside Israel to Bethlehem reminds us that God's love reaches all people everywhere and challenges us as a congregation to be a microcosm of God's diverse and worldwide family.

I would like to acknowledge my gratitude to the following people: The Rev. Dr. Peter Wiley, Senior Pastor and the Rev. Sue Ann Schmidt, Associate Pastor have inspired and guided me the past five years that I have spent on the staff of the First Congregational Church in Hudson, Ohio. The Rev. Dr. Dan Schomer, Executive Presbyter of the Eastminster Presbytery (Ohio) and the Rev. Rich Plant, Associate Association Minister of the Eastern Ohio Association (U.C.C.), have given me tremendous support through the years. The editorial staff of CSS Publishing Company, especially President David Runk and Missy Cotrell have skillfully steered me from beginning to end in making the publication of this book possible. Finally, I am indebted to my wife Arlene who has read the complete manuscript making many helpful suggestions and, as always, provides the encouragement I need at the right time.

---

1. George Linkbeck had a similar experience. See Robert E. Dunham, *Expecting God's Surprises* (Louisville, Kentucky: Geneva Press, 2001), 63-64.

Keeping Awake

Lehman's Old-Fashioned Hardware Store at Kidron in Ohio's Amish Country is a fascinating place. This store has specialized in non-electric appliances for more than forty years. Until recently most of its customers have been Amish residents in Holmes, Wayne, and Tuscarawas counties and Christian missionaries in countries of the developing world. The store is appealing to a growing number of religious people caught up in the so-called prophetic teaching that the last days are fast approaching. They have read about the store in books and on internet websites, and they are buying materials to prepare for what they believe will be disruptive times.

The Lehmans themselves are not worried about this being the end time, but apparently many other people are. I am with the Lehmans. I do not fear the future nor do I see it as our task to try to predict the date of Jesus' return or to signal out specific people who will be leading figures in the last day. Our biblical text today expresses clearly that no one knows when the end time will come; not even Jesus knew as he spoke to his disciples a short time before going to the cross. On the positive side Jesus does tell us how we should prepare for the last day, in fact prepare for every day. We do this by "keeping awake."

The gospel lectionary text for the First Sunday in Advent always centers not on the birth of Jesus in Bethlehem but upon Jesus' coming again in the future. Our particular passage describes his coming in dramatic fashion:

The sun will be darkened, and the moon will not give its light; the stars will be falling from heaven, and the powers in the heavens will be shaken.

— Mark 13:24-25

Jesus then tells a parable of the fig tree signifying that "summer is near" — a time of promise, fulfillment, and hope.

The biblical passage concludes with another parable in which Jesus tells of a man going on a journey who leaves his servants in charge while he is gone. They do not know when he will return. The doorkeeper is commanded to be on the watch. The only way the servants can be sure of their master's praise when he returns is to be on constant watch. This does not mean they sit around doing nothing and only scan the horizon. No, they are to do their assigned tasks with faithfulness. If they do that, they need not know the precise time when their master will return.

Jesus concludes the story by speaking to his disciples and saying, "What I say to you I say to all: Keep awake" (Mark 13:37).

These words anticipate the poignant failure of the disciples to stay awake in the Garden of Gethsemane when Jesus goes off alone to pray. Each time he returns he finds his disciples sleeping even though he had asked them to stay awake. (Compare Mark 14:32-42.)

Other references in the gospels confirm Jesus' warning. Matthew elaborates more in his account and spells out the consequences of not keeping watch in graphic detail (Matthew 24:36-51). Matthew also follows up this section that is similar to Mark with a new parable of the wise and foolish maidens underscoring the same point. Luke in his gospel concludes with a similar challenge: "You must be ready for the Son of Man is coming at an unexpected hour" (Luke 12:35-40).

What do Jesus' words have to say specifically to us as we enter the Advent season? Despite Jesus' explicit warning not to be concerned about the date and the details when the last day will arrive, some of his followers in every generation since the first century have sought to determine when this cataclysmic event is going to take place.

One of the most bizarre examples of misplaced fervor happened in the 1840s in western New York. This time and place has frequently been called "The Burned-over District" because of the repeated religious revivals that occurred during the first part of the nineteenth century. William Miller studied biblical prophecy and he was certain from his calculations that Jesus would return on March 21, 1843. Many of his followers went out into the open fields or gathered on the hilltop to await this spectacular event. Nothing happened!

Miller, not deterred by this huge disappointment, went back to his calculations and figured he had made a few mistakes but finally he arrived at a new date that he felt was absolutely correct, namely October 22, 1844. Once again nothing happened. He and his followers ultimately became disillusioned with their fanatical adventism.[1]

Even in our own generation prophetic teaching abounds. Ever since the state of Israel was formed in 1948 prophetic teachers have become more certain than ever that we are living in the last days. In their interpretation of the scriptures the major events leading up to Jesus' return will take place in the land that is now the state of Israel. Some predictors set definite dates; others set a date just a few years ahead hoping if it is not the right date, people will forget about the original forecast. In the meantime, not a few people are filled with extraordinary expectation or dread.

In addition to date setting, it is common among such "prophetic" teachers to single out particular world personalities and associate them with symbolic figures in the gospels, the letters of Paul, or the book of Revelation. In my lifetime I have heard so many speak with certainty that the Anti-Christ was Hitler, Stalin, Mao, Saddam Hussein, or whoever happens to be the current dictator of choice.

Not long ago one of our most prominent TV evangelists claimed the gigantic computer in Belgium used to process information in the world financial markets actually is the "Beast" mentioned in the book of Revelation. Someday, the TV evangelist warned, the computer will fall into the wrong hands and wreck the world economy leading to chaos and eventually to the final battle of Armageddon.

As G.K. Chesterton, the British wit of another generation, once remarked: "... though Saint John the evangelist saw many strange monsters in his vision, he saw no creatures so wild as one of his own commentators."[2]

Rather than seeking to predict definite dates or try to relate current personalities with the symbols of the apocalyptic sections of the scriptures in contradiction to Jesus' explicit command, how much better to continue with our assigned tasks of discipleship whatever they be with faithfulness.

One of the best ways we can maintain a balance and not go off on tangents in the midst of the current world's uncertainty and unrest is to worship regularly and have our worship guided by the festivals and seasons of the Christian year. In this way, we will stay close to Jesus, our Lord, and not be distracted by the latest fashionable fad in the deceptive domain of prophecy.

In Walker Percy's novel, *The Second Coming*, he describes one of his characters in this manner: "Not once in his entire life had he allowed himself to come to rest in the quiet center of himself but had forever cast himself forward from some dark past he could not remember to a future which did not exist. Not once had he been present for his life. So his life had passed like a dream."[3]

We do not want to be like this man. We want to keep awake, not worrying about the details of the end time but focusing upon the present. We are looking for God's next visit, whether or not it is God's last visit. "Keeping awake" is the hope of the Advent season. Amen.

---

1. Whitney R. Cross, *The Burned-over District: The Social and Intellectual History of Enthusiastic Religion in Western New York, 1800-1850* (New York: Harper & Row Publishers, 1950), 287-321.

2. G.K. Chesterton, *Orthodoxy* (New York: John Lane Co., 1908), 29.

3. Walker Percy, *The Second Coming* (New York: Farrar, Straus & Giroux, 1980), 124.

Modeling Humility

As a young man Benjamin Franklin sought to attain moral perfection; consequently, he made a list of twelve virtues he thought would make up the good life. He devoted a page to each of these traits in a little book. Every page was ruled with seven lines, one for every day of the week. His plan was to give special attention to one of these twelve virtues at a time for a whole week, also making note of daily failures. He hoped thereby to train himself in a better way of life.

One day, Franklin showed his list to a Quaker friend in Philadelphia. This man pointed out what he thought Franklin needed most of all, namely he had forgotten to include "humility" among the virtues he sought to attain. Therefore, Franklin added it. His entire list read: temperance, silence, order, resolution, frugality, industry, sincerity, justice, moderation, cleanliness, tranquility, chastity, and humility. After the word "humility" Franklin wrote: imitate Socrates and Jesus.[1]

Many of us, like Benjamin Franklin, are apt to put "humility" last on our scale of virtues, if we list it at all, and yet a humble attitude might be what we need most to model in our personal lives.

A.M. Hunter, a Scottish New Testament scholar, distinguished the four gospel writers in their approach to telling the good news in the following manner. Matthew begins with an elaborate genealogy. Luke, who plans to write a literary gospel, prefaces his work with a prolegomena. John, like the eagle which is his emblem, soars at once into the theological skies with the eternal word. Mark simply puts down half a dozen blunt, important words by way of superscription and plunges forthwith into his narrative.[2]

Mark introduces John at the beginning of his gospel as the forerunner of the coming Messiah and at the heart of his proclamation are the words: "... The one who is more powerful than I is coming after me; I am not worthy to stoop down and untie the thong of his sandals" (Mark 1:7).

John the Baptist calls upon the people to take heed to his message that can change their lives. Mark combines two scripture references from the Hebrew Bible (Malachi 3:1; Isaiah 40:3) to sum up his message:

> See, I am sending my messenger ahead of you, who will prepare your way; the voice of one crying out in the wilderness: "Prepare the way of the Lord, make his paths straight."
>
> — Mark 1:2-3

In other words, just as God had redeemed the people of Israel out of their bondage in Egypt ages ago in the first exodus, a "new exodus" is opening up for those who have eyes to see. The multitude of seekers who came out to hear John undoubtedly identified with their ancestors who crossed over the Jordan River into the Promised Land under the leadership of Joshua many centuries before this date. Like these early Israelites they too were willing to embark on a new adventure responding to God's call. The Jordan River became a kind of frontier by which those who were willing to cross over entered into a new land of promise.

If we were there that day we too might have been caught up in the excitement of John's proclamation. We too might have been thrilled to see this strange wilderness prophet and join the throngs of people from the Judean hillside who flocked to hear him.

What a sight John was to behold. He was dressed like Elijah or one of the other Hebrew prophets in camel's hair with a leather belt around his waist. His diet consisted of "locusts and wild honey." It had been 400 long years since a genuine prophet had spoken to the people of Israel and they were all ears to hear what this man had to say.

What was John's message? It was a message of "repentance for the forgiveness of sins." Repentance means literally "to change your mind," "to change the direction in which you are going and go a different way." Repentance means "confessing your sins," being earnestly sorry for them. In so doing, those who repented put themselves in a position to receive God's forgiveness.

The sign that the people were really serious about starting a "new exodus" would be their willingness to be baptized in the Jordan River. We must note that this was only a preliminary baptism. The more important baptism would be the baptism of the Holy Spirit by the Messiah himself.

Therefore, it is plain to see that John's emphasis is not upon himself. Nor is the emphasis even upon his ministry. He is not important but Jesus is the all-important one. John makes it abundantly clear that he is only a messenger who points to the one who is more powerful than he is.

Our relationship with God is not based on any merit of our own. God does not enter into a relationship with us because we are good. Recall that the ancient prophets as well as John the Baptist reminded the people that God loved them not because they were great or good, but God loved Israel. Period. God has the same love for each one of us and calls us into a loving and forgiving bond of friendship. We can ignore God's call, but God's persistent love continues to beat upon our door.

The good news of the gospel does not say, "Trust God, and he will love you," but rather the gospel message says, "God already loves you, so trust him," a subtle but important difference.

Not a few preachers who have gone to supply a pulpit on a given Sunday in another town have had the experience of mounting the pulpit getting ready to preach and noticing a plaque staring them in the face with the words, "Sir, we wish to see Jesus." That is what the congregation wishes to see in the message to be proclaimed, and that is exactly what John told his followers who came out to see him. He gave them Jesus.

Likewise today, we all need to model the humility that John the Baptist exhibited.

Peter Marshall, Chaplain of the United States Senate during the 1940s purportedly once gave this prayer at the opening session of the Senate:

> O God, so long have we been riding on the balloon tires of conceit, for our good we may have to be deflated, that on the rims of humility we may discover spiritual laws that govern our growth in grace. If our pride has been punctured, Lord, make it soon before we gain too much speed.[3]

The prayer seems relevant for us today too.

When we think of ourselves too highly we ought to remember that the number of people who attend our funeral will in large part depend upon how hard it is raining at that time.

Hans Kung, the ecumenical Roman Catholic theologian, has always been a great admirer of Karl Barth, the Swiss Reformed scholar, arguably the most prominent theologian of the twentieth century. One day when Kung was a young man, he visited Barth at his home in Basel, Switzerland. Kung could not stop praising the older man for all the profound books Barth had written and for his amazing grasp of the Christian faith.

Finally, Barth turned to the youthful Kung and said, "When one day I am called before God, I will not come with all my collected theological works in an Alper-Hutte (rucksack) on my back; all the angels will laugh. Nor will I say in justification of myself, 'I always had good intentions, good faith.' No, I will stand there with empty hands and only find appropriate those words which I hope may also be my own last words, 'God, be gracious to me a sinner!' "[4]

We cannot do much better than Barth. That should be our plea too.

One of the basic principles of AA (Alcoholics Anonymous) is that one practices humility, a complete dependence upon a Higher Power. The assumption is that we cannot help ourselves; we must be subject completely to someone else. We need humility, total honesty, a radical dependence upon a Higher Power, the one we call God.

If we were to attend the opening session of the General Assembly of the Church of Scotland we probably would be shocked at the treatment the Queen or her representative would receive. Although the Queen or her representative holds the title of Lord High Commissioner and resides in the palace of Holyrood House in Edinburgh, when that person comes to the opening of the General Assembly he or she is simply ignored at first. The rudeness is calculated to put that person in his or her place as an invited guest, an observer. Her Majesty the Queen may rule Britannia, but she does not rule the Church of Scotland.

That bit of symbolism displayed each time the Assembly meets underscores for those fiercely independent Scots that Jesus Christ alone is the head of the Kirk of Scotland.[5]

John the Baptist had the same spirit. He wanted nothing to stand in the way of exalting Jesus as Lord. His humility is a style worth modeling for all of us today. Amen.

———————

1. Benjamin Franklin, *Autobiography, & Selections from His Writings* (New York: Random House, Inc., 1944), 93-95, 103.

2. A.M. Hunter, *Saint Mark* (London: SCM PRESS LTD, 1955), 25.

3. *The Prayers of Peter Marshall* edited and with Prefaces by Catherine Marshall (New York: McGraw-Hill Book Company, Inc., 1949), 182.

4. Hans Kung, *My Struggle for Freedom: Memoirs* (Grand Rapids: William B. Eerdmans Publishing Company, 2002), 146.

5. Paul Carlson, *Our Presbyterian Heritage* (Elgin, Illinois: David C. Cook Publishing Co., 1973), 72-73.

Testifying to the Light

Edmund Morris, in the first volume of his brilliant trilogy, *The Rise of Theodore Roosevelt*, poignantly writes of Theodore's first wife Alice and his devotion to her. Alice Hathaway Lee was a striking beauty and only seventeen years old when Theodore met her. In his diary he recorded: "As long as I live, I shall never forget how sweetly she looked, and how prettily she greeted me." On October 27, 1880, they were married in Brookline, Massachusetts. All that Theodore could pen in his diary after the wedding was a terse comment, "Our intense happiness is too sacred to be written." They had a brief honeymoon and then they took up formal residence in New York City while Theodore registered to study at Columbia Law School.

Roosevelt was elected to the New York Assembly in 1882. On February 13, 1884, he received a telegram with the happy news that his wife Alice had given birth to a baby girl the night before. But several hours later, he received a second telegram indicating that she was dying and his mother who lived in the same house was dying too. Alice died of Bright's disease and his mother of acute typhoid fever. The two women closest to him died within hours of each other.

Theodore drew a cross in his diary for February 14, 1884, and wrote beneath, "The light has gone out of my life."[1]

We all have experienced darkness too, perhaps not such a double-barreled grief at the same time as Theodore suffered, but we all have undoubtedly said similar words at one time or another. We may have lost our way and cannot find the right direction. We may be having difficulty making decisions, worried about making the wrong choice. We may have little self-esteem — feeling we will never amount to anything. We may even be in such despair that we have become convinced that no one cares for us, not even God, if there is one. Yes, we have known darkness too.

Even the intrepid wilderness pioneer Daniel Boone had his moments. Once when he had been asked if he had ever been lost, "No," he replied slyly, "but I was bewildered once for three days."[2] We probably have been bewildered more often than that in our own lifetimes.

Our gospel reading today speaks to us if we sense we are walking in darkness. The gospel of John had much to say about light in contrast to darkness. John the Baptist in this scripture passage is portrayed as one who comes to bear witness, "to testify to the light, so that all might believe through him." He is adamant that he is not the light, "but he came to testify to the light. The true light, which enlightens everyone, was coming into the world" (John 1:7-9).

Light is a prominent symbol in the Hebrew Bible as well as in the New Testament. Light was associated with God and with the Law of Moses. The Psalmist declared:

> The Lord is my light and my salvation; whom shall I fear? The Lord is the stronghold of my life; of whom shall I be afraid?
>
> — Psalm 27:1

The psalmist also associated light with the Law.

> Your word is a lamp to my feet and a light to my path.
>
> — Psalm 119:105

The prophets also equated light with God's protection:

> The sun shall no longer be your light by day, nor for brightness shall the moon give light to you by night;

22

but the Lord will be your everlasting light, and your
God will be your glory.

— Isaiah 60:19

… when I sit in darkness, the Lord will be a light to
me.

— Micah 7:8

As we read the gospel of John it soon becomes apparent
that John the Baptist is not hesitant in referring to Jesus as the
light. Later, Jesus himself in one of his great "I am" sayings,
makes this startling promise: "I am the light of the world.
Whoever follows me will never walk in darkness but will
have the light of life" (John 8:12).

These words were enunciated in the context of one of
the major festivals of the Jewish people, namely the Feast
of the Tabernacles. Jesus was present in Jerusalem when this
annual festival took place to remember God's providence in
guiding the people of Israel through the desert eventually
leading them to the Promised Land. God guided his people
with a pillar of cloud during the day and a pillar of fire at
night (Exodus 13:21-22). These signs symbolized God's
presence with them at all times.

During the festival in Jerusalem four huge candelabra
were placed in the center of the Court of the Women in the
Temple for all to see. When the candles were lit, the singing
and dancing began. It was within such a setting that Jesus
walked into the joyful celebration and announced his own
identification with God's light.

We also recall from Jesus' words in the Sermon on the
Mount that he called his disciples "the light of the world." It
was not so much that his followers would produce their own
light, but rather the light they had was a borrowed or reflected
light. As they stayed close to Jesus, they had a radiance that
was noticeable to others. The purpose of his disciples letting
their light shine before the world was not to call attention

23

to themselves but rather that they may see your good works "and give glory to your Father in heaven" (Matthew 5:16).

Even the smallest glimmer of light can work wonders — if Jesus is connected to it.

The Rev. Dr. Peter Wiley tells of vivid childhood memories related to Christmas Eve services. The most vivid memory goes back to the time when he was a bearer of the Christ Candle at the age of twelve. He recalls his neo-gothic church with a long slate center aisle. He carried two lighters with him in case the candle blew out — one in his hand and another in his pocket, just in case.

He goes on to say that one little burning wick doesn't seem like much, until you burn that one candle in an absolutely darkened space. One little candle doesn't seem like much, until you carry a candle with 2,000 eyes watching. Then, he says, that one little candle is absolutely blinding.

Reflecting on that Christmas Eve experience he contrasts that little light with what we would do if we had a dinner party. We would burn lots ands lots of candles to light up the room. Just one candle doesn't seem to be enough, but on Christmas Eve in the midst of a darkened sanctuary, we get to see the single candle and it brings light to everyone.

Peter draws to a close his recollections by saying: "A funny thing about carrying the Christ Candle is that you can't tell how much light it's bringing to everyone else. When the light is right in front of you it seems so very small. Rather pathetic, to be honest. And that single light right in front of your eyes blinds you to everything else. Does one light ever make a real difference? Sometimes it makes a difference without you even knowing it."[3]

Jesus, "the light of the world," continues to speak to those who struggle in darkness. He speaks to the ones who have lost their way and points them to the way. He speaks to the ones who are frustrated in their decision-making and challenges them to take up their cross and follow him. He speaks to the ones with low self-esteem and reveals to them the God who says, "This is my Son, the Beloved, with whom I am well pleased" (Matthew 3:17). Finally, he speaks to the ones who feel that no one cares for them, not even God, and he reminds them that God has been seeking them even before they had a thought about God.

Dr. John Vanarsdall once shared this story that has its setting around 1800 in New England. A child by the name of John Todd was born in Vermont. When he was only six years old both his parents died, and he was sent to live with an aunt who took exceptionally good care of him. She sacrificed and enabled him to go to college and enter one of the professions. Later in his adult life John learned that his aunt was seriously ill and that she was terrified of dying. He lived in another part of the country and could not easily get to see his aunt in her final days. Therefore, he decided to write a letter and this is what he said:

"It is now 35 years since I, a little boy of six, was left quite alone in the world. I have never forgotten that day when I made the long journey to your house in North Killingsworth. I still recall how you sent your hired man Caesar to fetch me. And I can still remember my tears and anxiety as, perched on your horse and clinging tightly to Caesar's back, I started out for my new home. As we rode along, I became more and more afraid and finally said to Caesar, 'Do you think she will go to bed before we get there?' 'Oh, no,' he said reassuringly. 'When we get out of these here woods, you will see her candle shining in the window.'

"In a short time, we did ride out into a clearing, and there, sure enough, was your candle. I still remember the sight of you waiting at the door, how you put out your arms to me and lifted me down from the horse. I remember there was a fire on your hearth, a warm supper on your stove, and after supper, you took me up to bed, heard my prayers, and then sat beside me until I dropped off to sleep.

"You undoubtedly realize why I am recalling all these things just now. Some day soon, God may send for you to take you to a new home. Do not fear that summons, and do not fear the strange journey or the messenger of death. At the end of the road you will find love and welcome. You will be safe in God's love and care. Surely God can be trusted to be as kind to you there as you were to me years ago."[4]

Jesus, "the light of the world," assures us that at the end there will be a "candle in the window" awaiting us as well. Amen.

---

1. Edmund Morris, *The Rise of Theodore Roosevelt* (New York: Random House Trade Paperbacks, 2010), 230.
2. Philip Cousineau, *The Art of Pilgrimage: The Seeker's Guide to Making Travel Sacred* (Berkeley: Conari, 1998), 156.
3. Sermon preached by the Rev. Dr. Peter Wiley at First Congregational Church U.C.C., Hudson, Ohio, February 6, 2011.
4. As told by the Reverend John R. Claypool in a sermon published in the *Biblical Preaching Journal* (Spring, 1990, Volume 3), 23.

Believing the Impossible

There are a lot of good things to say about being a parent or a grandparent and one of the joys is that we get a chance to read children's stories. Recently, I read *Through the Looking Glass and What Alice Saw There* by Lewis Carroll. I especially liked the conversation between the Queen and Alice when the little girl complained to the Queen, "But I find it impossible to believe what you say." At which her majesty grumbled, "Well, maybe you do, my dear, but when I was your age I made it a point to believe six impossible things before breakfast."[1]

Do we have a problem believing impossible things? Not six impossible things before breakfast, but do we have a problem with even one impossible thing?

Mary was caught up in an impossible situation and yet she believed.

It is a familiar story we have heard many times. The angel Gabriel appeared to Mary who lived in the obscure village of Nazareth in Galilee. She was engaged to a man named Joseph of the house of David. Gabriel's message to Mary was, "Greetings, favored one! The Lord is with you" (Luke 1:28). Mary is perplexed by the announcement. The angel calms her with the words, "Do not be afraid, Mary, for you have found favor with God. And now you will conceive in your womb and bear a son, and you will name him Jesus" (Luke 1:30-31). Gabriel goes on to say that Mary's son will be called great and be called "Son of the Most High" and he will be given the throne of his ancestor, King David. His kingdom will be eternal (Luke 1:32-33).

We probably should pause here before hearing Mary's reply to note that Gabriel did not spell out all the details of being "the favored one." Being called the favored one did not mean that Mary was to have a life of peace with no problems or pain. The very fact that the birth of her child raised questions in the minds of many people meant that she was to have a rough start in her marriage to Joseph. Although her son did become popular and was held in high esteem by many of the faithful, he soon encountered much criticism. In the end Mary had to bear the embarrassment and agony of the arrest, trial, and death upon the cross of her beloved son. Only as we look back through the lens of the resurrection do we grasp the full meaning of Gabriel's words: "Do not be afraid, Mary, for you have found favor with God."

Return to Mary's immediate response, "How can this be, since I am a virgin?" Then Gabriel explains further, "the Holy Spirit will come upon you…" He goes on to say that her cousin Elizabeth, in her old age, has conceived a son. This has been a miracle too. Gabriel ends the conversation by reminding Mary, "For nothing will be impossible with God" (Luke 1:34-37).

These words are similar to the divine message to Abraham after Sarah, his wife, had laughed when told that she would have a child in old age. God's word came to Abraham and Sarah, "Is anything too wonderful for the Lord?" (Genesis 18:14).

Mary's response to this strange message was, "Here am I, the servant of the Lord; let it be with me according to your word" (Luke 1:38).

We are dealing with a mystery that cannot easily be described. Only Luke and Matthew mention the birth of Jesus, and they do not refer to it later in their gospels. The apostle Paul does not comment upon the virgin birth of Jesus. For Paul and the writers of the four gospels, Jesus' resurrection is the central affirmation.

However we interpret this mystery, N.T. Wright, the English New Testament scholar and prolific writer, reminds us: "… we shouldn't miss the contrast between muddled, puzzled Zechariah in the previous story in Luke and the obedient humility of Mary in this one."[2]

Though the message seemed impossible for Mary to accept, nonetheless, she believed.

Mary from a backwater village in Galilee has become a symbol of obedient faith. How often we miss the extraordinary in the midst of the ordinary.

The Flemish artist Pieter Bruegel of the early seventeenth century painted a magnificent picture titled "The Numbering in Bethlehem." He interprets Luke's story by depicting the characters in a typical Flemish village. We see the snow on the ground contrasting with the color brown throughout the painting. We notice the frozen pond and the children frolicking on the ice. The other villagers seem to be going about their daily chores. Handcarts are parked in front of the village inn, and a Christmas wreath hangs on the wall of the inn.

As we survey the painting with its exquisite detail, we almost miss a man approaching the village with a donkey and a young woman in tow off the side. Bruegel pictures Mary and Joseph making their way to the inn on just an ordinary day in an ordinary town.[3]

How frequently we look for important things in the wrong places. We can be so enamored with what appears to be the more exciting persons and events that we miss the most important truth of all.

Jim had an idea for a television show that might appeal to children. He had some success on a local television show. He approached the major networks — ABC, CBS, and NBC — with this idea of a family variety series. They turned him down, each one of them. Eventually, he found someone in

England who thought his idea had a chance of catching on. In 1976 the show was put into world distribution.

To be sure, we might have been skeptical at first. It might have been hard to believe that a show featuring an uneasy green frog, a royal-blue monster with an insatiable appetite for cookies, and a big, curious, naïve, vulnerable, sympathetic golden bird would have a wide appeal.

Today, we know that Jim Henson's idea of the Muppets on "Sesame Street" has become one of the greatest shows of all time. It is likely that more people can name the Muppet pig "Miss Piggy" who is in love with the Muppet frog Kermit than they can name the capital of Afghanistan.

It is simply amazing what God can do with a person who seems so ordinary if that person chooses to be available.

Maya Angelou, an American poet who has been our poet laureate, read her poetry at a presidential inauguration. She continues to challenge the conscience of our nation and tells how a friend long ago helped her to see she was someone God could use. In her autobiographical *Wouldn't Take Nothing for My Journey* she tells her story.

"One day the teacher Frederick Wilkerson asked me to read to him. I was 24, very erudite, very worldly. He asked that I read from the book, *Lessons in Truth*, a section that ended with the words: 'God loves me.'

"I read the piece and closed the book, and the teacher said, 'Read it again.' I pointedly opened the book, and I sarcastically read, 'God loves me.' He said, 'Again.' After about the seventh repetition I began to sense that there might be truth in the statement and that there was a possibility that God really did love me. Me, Maya Angelou.

"I suddenly began to cry at the grandness of it all. I knew that if God loved me, then I could do wonderful things. I could try great things, learn anything. For what could stand against me with God, since one person, any person, with God constitutes a majority."[4]

"She is a remarkable woman," we say to ourselves, "but I am just an ordinary person." How often if we look close enough and hard enough we will find that some ordinary people can do extraordinary things.

As part of my responsibilities in recent years I have spent quite a bit of time visiting in a retirement home. Retired people are frequently classified as "old-young" if they are in their sixties or seventies and they are "old-old" if they are in their eighties or nineties. Many of the people I have visited are in the latter category, in particular those who are in the medical center of the retirement home. At first glance the men and women look pretty much alike. Most of them cannot function very well because of their physical and mental conditions, but when you begin to talk with them in some depth, you hear captivating stories.

As the residents reflect upon their early years I learn that they are a diverse group including: artists, bankers, bookbinders, homemakers, lawyers, librarians, mission workers, physicians, shipbuilders, and teachers to name a few vocations. They all have extraordinary memories of how God has guided them through the years in their varied work places and family life.

Such visits have convinced me we all have spiritual journeys worth sharing with others.

Tony Campolo has taught sociology at Eastern College at St. Davids, just outside Philadelphia for many years. He is a Baptist preacher as well and a well-known conference speaker. Tony has a special passion to help inner-city kids who live in "the projects."

One day he had what he thought was a brilliant idea. As he observed kids playing in a church-sponsored basketball league, he came up with the idea that he would have them play an exhibition game with some of the players on the Philadelphia Eagles professional football team. In the off-season these professional football players try to keep in shape by playing basketball.

You can imagine how excited the boys were when Tony told them of his plans. The game would be played in the Eastern College gym. In this setting Tony was hoping that at least some of the kids would get a desire to go to college some day, and he would help them financially. Before the big game Tony gathered his players together to give them a pep talk. All of them seemed to be listening attentively.

Then, from out of nowhere Tony heard the harsh voice of their coach interrupting Tony's pep talk. The coach had grown up in the projects, and he had volunteered to help the boys. He shouted, "Don't listen to him. Guys like him are always coming along and promising you they can get you out of the projects. Don't listen. People like him used to tell me the same thing. I tried and tried, and it didn't do me any good. Look at me. I'm still here, ain't I? And you're gonna be there when you're my age too. So you better get used to being in the projects and don't pay any attention to what he says."

There was dead silence following that outburst. The kids just sat there hanging their heads. Tony didn't know what to say at first but he was one who was never lost for words for very long. He then quoted a brief poem, the essence of which was to encourage his young friends not to give up but to believe in the impossible. Even though the coach was unimpressed with Tony's pep talk, these young people might be able to do more than they ever dreamed possible. Anything was possible for them. They should not listen to anyone who was negative about their potential because they had their whole lives ahead of them and who knows what they could achieve given the right motivation and support. The kids looked straight at Tony. Then he said, "Okay, now let's play ball."

The coach had been hurt. His dreams were all faded and just about forgotten. It was painful for him, but he had no right to keep those kids from dreaming. Without dreams, kids die.[5]

That applies to us all. Anything **can** happen. Believing the impossible is the way God uses ordinary people to do extraordinary things. Amen.

---

1. "Through the Looking Glass and What Alice Saw There," *The Complete Illustrated Works of Lewis Carroll* (New York: Avenel Books, 1982), 127-128.

2. Tom Wright, *Luke for Everyone* (Louisville: Westminster John Knox Press, 2004), 12.

3. William H. Willimon, *On a Wild and Windy Mountain* (Nashville: Abingdon Press, 1984), 15-17.

4. Maya Angelou, *Wouldn't Take Nothing for My Journey Now* (New York: Random House, 1993), 75.

5. Tony Campolo, *Carpe Diem: Seize the Day* (Dallas: Word Publishing, 1994), 93-95.

Distinguishing Between Disaster and Blessing

There is an old Taoist story about a wise man who lived on the northern frontier of China. One day, for no apparent reason, a young man's horse ran away and was taken by nomads across the border. Everyone tried to console the young man for his ill fortune, but his father, a wise man, said, "What makes you so sure this is not a blessing?"

Months later, his horse returned, bringing with her a magnificent stallion. This time everyone was full of congratulations for the son's good fortune. However, his father said, "What makes you so sure this isn't a disaster?" Their house was made richer by this fine horse, which his son loved to ride. One day he fell off the horse and broke his hip. Once again, everyone offered consolations for his bad luck, but his father said, "What makes you so sure this is not a blessing?"

A year later the nomads mounted an invasion across the border and every able-bodied man was required to take up his bow and go into battle. The Chinese frontiersmen lost nine of every ten men. Only because the son was lame did father and son survive to take care of each other. Truly, the story reminds us blessing turns to disaster and disaster to blessing.[1]

The Christmas story in the gospel of Luke could be viewed from one angle as a disaster but from another angle it seems to be a blessing. Using our imagination we can picture Joseph and his pregnant wife Mary starting out on their eighty-mile journey from Nazareth to Bethlehem. What a difficult trip it must have been. Once they arrived in Bethlehem they were to discover no lodging accommodations were available except for a stable in back of the inn or possibly underneath the house itself. Here they were alone, knowing not a single person, and their son is born in less than hygienic and comfortable surroundings.

The first people to greet them were not the dignitaries of the town but rough-looking, smelly shepherds from the hillside who claimed to have received word that the Messiah was to be born in Bethlehem that very night. In first-century Palestine the shepherds were considered to be on the lower level of the social scale. To be sure, Joseph and Mary might have recalled that King David had been a shepherd, but Luke probably includes them in this story because his purpose in writing his gospel is to show that God's good news in Jesus reached out in a special way to the poor, despised, and outcasts of society, even to lowly shepherds tending their sheep on lonely hilltops.

Everything seemed to have gone wrong for Joseph and Mary. Surely they might have thought of this night as a disaster.

From our own perspective of 2,000 years we interpret the birth of Jesus, though born in humble circumstances, not to be a disaster but a blessing. A Savior has been born, the long-awaited Messiah, the hope of Israel, the Lord. Hence the angelic host sang: "Glory to God in the highest heaven, and on earth peace among those whom he favors" (Luke 2:14).

Likewise, the death of Jesus would be seen as a tragic disaster at first. When Charlemagne, king of the Franks during the Middle Ages, first heard the story of Jesus' arrest and execution, he exploded in rage. Seizing his sword, he shouted for all to hear, "Oh, if only I had been there; I would have slain them all with my legions!" We can appreciate the ardent faith of this follower of Jesus but we wonder what he could have done if he had been there. God was present at the cross but did not intervene. Jesus himself claimed he could have called on an army of angels but he did not ask for help either. Jesus had told his disciples earlier: "No one has greater love than this, to lay down one's life for one's friends" (John 15:13). God's way was not to display power but to disclose love, sacrificial love, and this has ever been the appeal of the good news. After the resurrection Jesus' followers understood his death not to be a disaster but the greatest blessing of all.[2]

Throughout history what at first was thought to be a disaster has in the end been called a blessing. Consider the American Revolution and George Washington's crucial role as the commanding General for the Patriot side. If we were to total up victories in the various battles of the war, Washington would be labeled a weak General at best. He lost most of the individual battles he fought. He almost lost his whole army in the engagement at New York, but it was his good fortune that a heavy fog rolled across the Brooklyn shore enabling his 9,000 men to escape the British troops in the nick of time. After that Washington had few victories except for surprise raids at Trenton and at Princeton. For the most part he skillfully retreated to avoid a direct confrontation with the larger and more experienced British soldiers. Washington was handicapped by a Continental Congress that did not provide adequate funds or soldiers for him to take the offensive. Later in the war he lost battles at Brandywine and Germantown. Finally, in 1781, six years into the war, Washington prevailed assisted by French troops and more importantly by the French fleet that blockaded the harbor at Yorktown, Virginia, so that Cornwallis and his British troops were trapped with no escape possible. Victory at Yorktown became the decisive battle of the war. Up to this point disaster seemed to be the verdict of the Patriot cause, but when all was over Washington's courage, patience, and strong leadership carried the day. Even in the dark days of the winter at Valley Forge, Washington's closest military advisors saw in their General something that would carry them through although odds seemed to be against them. Henry Knox confided in Washington: "The people of America look up to you as their father, and into your hands they entrust their all, fully confident of every exertion on your part for their security and happiness."[3] It was that confidence and trust that in the course of time would turn disaster into blessing.

An episode in my own life has convinced me that I commonly do not know what is best for me. I had been serving a church as an interim pastor for three years when the search committee reported that it was ready to recommend a candidate to the congregation as pastor. I was told the candidate was "absolutely sure" he was ready to respond to the call and begin his pastoral duties.

About the same time all of this was happening I was contacted by another church to see if I would come to be their interim pastor. I really wanted to go to this church and I was happy to receive an invitation even though it was thought to be a brief interim period. Then disaster struck, at least it seemed that way to me. At the last minute the prospective candidate decided not to come. What was I to do? I had served in this current church for three years as the interim pastor. I was ready to accept a new assignment. My wife Arlene, who has always been my spiritual and moral compass, pointed me in the right direction. She convinced me that as much I wanted to make a move my first responsibility was to stay where I was and complete the task. One of the most difficult things I have had to do was to call the chair of the interim pastor search committee and tell him I could not come right then and why I could not come.

I stayed another six months until the church did call a candidate who agreed to come and to this day he has had a fruitful pastorate. My wife and I worshiped in a number of churches during the summer and one Sunday we decided to worship at the church where I wanted to go as an interim pastor. By now they had a permanently installed pastor. In talking to the senior pastor I learned that they were looking for a part-time associate pastor. I did not know this when we visited the church. In the end I was asked to join their church staff. I served as an associate pastor for five delightful years.

If I had been able to accept the interim pastoral position in this church it only would have been for five months. As it turned out, I later went to the church and served not for five months but five years. What appeared like a disaster actually became for me an extraordinary blessing.

Those of us who live in the Midwest frequently take mini-vacation trips to Frankenmuth, Michigan, often titled "Michigan's Little Bavaria." The town is located just north of the city of Flint. A group of fifteen German-Lutheran missionaries came to the area in 1845 to share the Christian gospel with the Chippewa Indians. Frankenmuth means "Courage of the Franconians." "Muth" is the German word for courage, and "Franken" refers to Franconia, the region of Germany from which the settlers came.

Today the town of more than 4,000 people is a thriving community that takes great pride in preserving their German heritage. They are famous for good food with two huge family restaurants, cheese and sausage factories, and much more. But surely the major attraction for most people is Bronner's "CHRISTmas Wonderland" — advertised as the world's largest Christmas store with some five acres under one roof. People come from all over the country to shop here.

Toward the south end of the premises is the "Silent Night Memorial Chapel" — a replica of the original one in Oberndorf, Austria, where the carol "Silent Night, Holy Night" was first sung in the Church of St. Nicholas. The church was washed away in a later flood and the chapel was erected on the same site. Incidentally, Oberndorf is only ten miles north of Salzburg, Austria, the home of Mozart and the location for the movie, *The Sound of Music.*

After a visit to Austria, Wally Bronner gained permission to build his "Silent Night Memorial Chapel" according to the original specifications of the one in Austria. As you move along the tranquil lamppost-lined walking path leading to the chapel you observe plaques with the hymn "Silent Night" written in 300 different languages. The peaceful interior of the chapel is an ideal place for prayer and meditation, a place to contemplate the deeper meaning of Jesus' birth.

The story behind the writing of this favorite Christmas carol is entrancing indeed!

Pastor Joseph Mohr of the newly erected Church of St. Nicholas learned only a few days before Christmas Eve from his organist Franz Gruber that the church organ had broken down. The people of this congregation had always looked forward to organ music on Christmas Eve.

To ease the tension Mohr decided to bundle himself up in his warmest winter clothes and visit members of his congregation. Shortly after he arrived at the home of one of his faithful families, a new baby was born to the poor laborer and his wife. Returning home he kept thinking about this newborn and also the coincidence of being born so close to Jesus' own birthday. When he arrived home, Pastor Mohr looked over some old notes he had made hoping to compose a poem. He finished his notes and the result was the words we now know as the beautiful Christmas carol:

> Silent Night, Holy Night
> All is calm, All is bright
> Round yon Virgin Mother and Child.
> Holy Infant, so tender and mild;
> Sleep in heavenly peace, Sleep in heavenly peace.

The next day Mohr saw Gruber again and showing him his slip of paper with the words he had just written, he asked his organist if he couldn't come up with music that would fit these words. Mohr offered his own guitar as a substitute for the church organ. Gruber did not exactly relish his task but he worked on it and by the time the Christmas Eve service rolled around, he had music to go with the pastor's words.

We are not certain whether it was Mohr or Gruber who played the guitar that night, but in any event, this congregation was the first group of people to sing "Stille Nacht. Heilge Nacht." In the spring the master organ repairman came around and did repair the church organ. While he was in Oberndorf, Mohr asked Gruber to play the new Christmas carol for him. The master organ repairman was so impressed he circulated the carol around Austria and Germany. Later it was further popularized by four Strasser sisters, one of the most acclaimed singing groups of the day. Eventually, this song was sung all over the world and has become one of our favorites, if not *the* favorite Christmas carol of all.[4]

What was an apparent disaster at first turned out to be an opportunity to create the memorable Christmas carol "Silent Night, Holy Night" — one of our richest blessings of the season. Amen.

---

1. Wayne Muller, *Sabbath* (New York: Bantam Books, 2002), 187-188.

2. Ron Chernow, *Washington: A Life* (New York: The Penguin Press, 2010), 323-325.

3. Philip Yancey, *Disappointment with God* (Grand Rapids: Zondervan Publishing House, 1992), 119.

4. Albert Edward Bailey, *The Gospel in Hymns* (New York: Charles Scribner's Sons, 1952), 342-343.

Being Aware of What Is Happening

Every evening about sunset at a popular hotel on the island of Maui, a young Hawaiian walks to the edge of a nearby cliff and suddenly dives a hundred feet into the ocean below. Dinner guests of the hotel look forward to this spectacular ritual as this young man gracefully dives into the blue Pacific waters.

There is no announcement made that the event is going to happen. It takes place when the torches are being lighted for the evening's festivities. You need to pay attention or you will miss it.

More than one person has said, "I just turned around to say something to my wife, and I missed it."[1]

Simeon and Anna, two of the central figures in our biblical story today did not miss their golden opportunity. They had been waiting for years for such an event to occur. They had faithfully come to the temple day after day with the expectation that the Messiah would arrive some day.

We begin with the arrival of Mary and Joseph and the baby Jesus. What is clear is that this family honored the Law of Moses. Luke tells us in the story immediately preceding our Christmas text that the couple had brought Jesus to be circumcised on the eighth day after his birth according to the ancient Hebrew commandment.

Mary and Joseph came back to the temple again for the purification rites and the presentation of their first-born son to God, once again according to the Law of Moses. Luke mentions their sacrifice as two turtledoves or two young pigeons. This was a provision for the poor who could not afford a more expensive sacrifice, such as a lamb. As we have noted before Luke is concerned to show that the good news of the gospel was available to all people, including the poor, the women, and the outcasts of society.

What this incident underscores unmistakably is that Jesus' family honored and respected their Jewish tradition. We must keep in mind that all of Jesus' disciples were Jews. Likewise, all the New Testament writers were Jews with the exception of Luke. Judaism is the mother faith of Christianity. Therefore, there can never be any justification for anti-Semitism among the followers of Jesus of Nazareth. We are rooted and grounded in the Jewish tradition, and we should never forget our spiritual heritage.

Simeon and Anna, unlike most of the people who came to Jerusalem for the festivals, were constantly on the alert for even the slightest signs that the Messiah had arrived. Simeon is described as follows: "There was a man in Jerusalem whose name was Simeon; this man was righteous and devout, looking for the consolation of Israel" (Luke 2:25).

Not too long ago I was watching a television special titled *Jerusalem Stories*. One of the most unforgettable scenes depicted Jews at the "Wailing Wall." That solitary wall is the only thing left of the temple. It is the most sacred spot in old Jerusalem for devout Jews. They pray, sing, and cry at that spot where they believe the Messiah will appear some day.

That was the same place where Simeon had been waiting for many years. As Mary and Joseph ascended the temple steps, Simeon, moved by God's Spirit sensed that the time had come. Simeon asked to hold the baby. Probably Mary was reluctant to give the baby to him, but she did. Simeon then praised God by saying: "Master, now you are dismissing your servant in peace, according to your word; for my eyes have seen your salvation, which you have prepared in the presence of all peoples, a light for revelation to the Gentiles and for glory to your people Israel" (Luke 2:29-32).

In the liturgy of the church these words have come to be known as the "Nunc Dimittis" from the first two words of the Latin translation.

It also is true that after blessing the child Simeon gave Mary a warning saying: "This child is destined for the falling and the rising of many in Israel, and to be a sign that will be opposed so that the inner thoughts of many will be revealed — a sword will pierce your own soul too" (Luke 2:34-35).

Anna, the other notable character in the story is described as an older devout woman who had the gift of prophecy. She is a widow and throughout her life she had been fasting and praying night and day that before she dies she too may see the Messiah. From the moment she saw the child she knew he was the one, and she could not keep the news to herself. She told others who also were "looking for the redemption of Jerusalem." In a profound sense, both Simeon and Anna represented the best of all Israel who were anticipating the coming Messiah.

Simeon and Anna were attentive. Are we aware of what is happening around us today?

Elizabeth Browning's oft-quoted words are apropos:

> Earth's crammed with heaven,
> And every common bush afire with God;
> But only he who sees, takes off his shoes —
> The rest sit round it and pluck blackberries....

John Calvin, the Swiss Reformed pastor of the sixteenth century, suggests a way we might be more attentive viewing our world, namely by using spectacles. What are these spectacles? Just as people with weak vision are aided by spectacles to see more clearly, Calvin understands the scriptures to be a kind of spectacles that enables us to see the world more clearly. It is not so much that the scriptures add new content into the world but rather like glasses they correct our astigmatism so that our sight becomes lucid and we can perceive what was there all along.[2]

If we want to make a real New Year's resolution in the coming week, we might resolve to look at the world through the lens of the scriptures and correct our own astigmatism. If we do, we will see the world in a whole different light and we will have hope.

Charles Wesley wrote more than 6,000 hymns, and he did not mind having the hymns published for distribution. He did have a qualification, however, he did not want any changes made to the words of his hymns, not even one word. He was insistent upon his instructions. We can be grateful that one of his publishers did not pay attention to his strictures. When Charles originally wrote his popular Christmas carol, "Hark! the Herald Angels Sing," the first line read as follows: "Hark, how all welkin rings, Glory to the King of kings." The word "welkin" was an old English word for "the vault of heaven." George Whitefield, one of Charles' friends, when he published a collection of his hymns in 1753 improved the wording to the now "Hark! The Herald Angels Sing." We are forever indebted for Whitefield's willingness to challenge Charles Wesley's rigid instructions never to change one of his hymns.[3]

Annie Dillard is one of my favorite authors. If ever there was an attentive person who knew what was going on around her it was Annie. In her 1974 Pulitzer Prize winning book, *Pilgrim at Tinker Creek*, she tells of her year roaming the Virginia woods. One entry in her journal caught my eye because she wrote it about this time of year that we are now entering. She exclaimed: "It is still the first week in January, and I've got great plans. I've been thinking about seeing. There are lots of things to see, unwrapped gifts and free surprises."[4]

If we are patient and wait for God to speak to us, we can be certain that God will speak. But we must be attentive.

Frederick Buechner, the novelist, tells of attending worship after many years of never darkening the doors of the church. He was a young man not sure what he should do with his life. Should he be a teacher, should he go into business? He was not certain. He lived in New York City at the time and he heard of a preacher by the name of George Buttrick, pastor of the Madison Avenue Presbyterian Church. Buttrick had some odd quirks in his speaking delivery, but he was highly intelligent and eloquent. He held young Buechner spellbound. Sunday after Sunday he listened to Buttrick's every word.

In the year 1953 around the time of the coronation of Queen Elizabeth II, in one of his sermons Buttrick was contrasting Elizabeth's coronation with the coronation of Jesus in the life of faith that should take place with confession and tears. And Buttrick added, "with confession and tears, and then as God was and is my witness, *great laughter*, he said... and at the phrase *great laughter*, for reasons that I have never satisfactorily understood, the great wall of China crumbled and Atlantis rose up out of the sea, and on Madison Avenue, at 73rd Street, tears leapt from my eyes as though I had been struck across the face."[5]

That was the decisive turning point in Buechner's young life. Now he knew what he wanted to be.

Whether it be waiting for the coming of the Messiah as was the case with Simeon and Anna, or whether it be waiting for life's directions as was the case for Frederick Buechner, or whatever our great longing may be, it is apt to be found when we are attentive, listening, and constantly aware of what is happening around us and within us. Amen.

----

1. James W. Angell, *Learning to Manage Our Fears* (Nashville: Abingdon, 1981), 20-21.

2. John Calvin, *Institutes of the Christian Religion*, Volume 1, edited by John T. McNeill and translated by Ford Lewis Battles (Philadelphia: The Westminster Press, 1960), 70.

3. Robert J. Morgan, *Then Sings My Soul* (Nashville: Thomas Nelson Publishers, 2003), 49.

4. Annie Dillard, *Pilgrim at Tinker Creek* (New York: Harper Perennial Modern Classics, 1974), 17.

5. Frederick Buechner, *The Alphabet of Grace* (San Francisco: Harper & Row, Publishers, 1970), 43-44.

New Year's Day
Matthew 25:31-46

Expecting Surprises on Judgment Day

A number of years ago when I lived in upstate New York I belonged to a Rotary Club. This service club, like the Lions and Kiwanis clubs, seeks to serve the community in a number of practical ways. As Christmas approached each year, one of our Rotary Club projects was to help the Salvation Army with their bell ringing. In my recollection it always seemed to be a cold, bitter, snowy day when I was given my two-hour assignment to ring the bell. I took my turn in front of our largest department store in town. I felt a little self-conscious at first ringing the bell but I knew it was for a good cause.

As I think back now on all those people hurrying by on their way to shop here and there, I cannot recall any specific classification of people who stopped by to drop something in the kettle. Some were old, others were young. Some looked prosperous, others did not. I was usually surprised when someone did give a donation. I never expected that sort of person to do it.

You could not help but feel that God was present in the lives of many of the strangers who passed by but you never knew in advance just when God had moved someone to be generous. All the strangers looked alike. They were just ordinary people full of surprises.

In Jesus' parable about judgment day, surprises abound too. The sheep and the goats are separated, the sheep on the right, the goats on the left; the former blessed, the latter accursed.

49

In this story the test for entering the kingdom of God is how individuals respond to the hungry, the thirsty, the stranger, the naked, the sick, and the prisoner. The Son of Man says that he is present in each one of these people, but "the righteous" did not realize this fact. They asked in amazement never recognizing in any of these different encounters. He replies: "Truly I tell you, just as you did it to one of the least of these who are members of my family, you did it to me" (Matthew 25:40).

Likewise, those who do not enter the kingdom of God did not recognize that the Son of Man was present in "the least of these."

We must keep in mind that this scripture passage is a parable. Jesus also spoke of the importance of faith and other aspects of discipleship. Nonetheless, identifying with the hungry, the thirsty, the stranger, the naked, the sick, and the prisoner is exactly what Jesus did in his ministry. He not only taught compassion but he did something about it.

Surely, this parable is disturbing to those of us who do not like surprises. We would prefer to have everything spelled out in black and white — what to believe, how to worship, what kind of church structure is best. In other words, not a few of us would like a set plan to guide our way. We like to know who is *in* and who is *out*.

It can be upsetting to us when we are forced to re-define our boundaries. Yet if nothing else, this parable persuades us that Jesus would extend our boundaries to include those who are hurting among, the hungry, the friendless, all those who are in need of comfort and healing. Even as Jesus moves among "the least of these" he impels us to do the same.

In this scripture passage, Jesus is depicted as the "Son of Man" referring to the last days. He is "king" suggesting his association with King David and the promised Messiah. He is "Lord" — not Caesar nor anyone else is lord. Finally, he is called "Judge," who will have the final say.

While keeping in mind this is a parable, we cannot escape the fact that this is the only detailed picture of the last judgment that Jesus gives us and it has nothing to do with rigid theology but simply the paramount criterion is how we act toward people in need.

During the late Middle Ages an unctuous monk by the name of Richard of Devizes warned innocent people who might be planning a visit to the city of London to beware of certain people:

> Do not associate with the crowds of pimps; do not mingle with the throngs in the eating-houses; avoid the dice and gambling, the theatre and the tavern. You will meet with more braggarts there than in all France; the number of parasites is infinite. Actors, jesters, smooth-skinned lads, Moors, flatterers, pretty boys, effeminates, pederasts, singing and dancing girls, quacks, belly-dancers, sorceresses, extortionists, night-wanderers, magicians, mimes, beggars, buffoons; all this tribe fill all the houses.[1]

The more you think about this list the more you realize that many of these people were the very people Jesus was criticized for associating with in his ministry. He loved to be with the outcasts and to welcome them into the kingdom of God.

Francis of Assisi in his early twenties was a delicate and fastidious young man. He always had a horror of dirt, smells, and mutilation of any kind. He especially shrank from lepers when he passed them along the highway. In fact, when he did encounter a leper he turned aside his face, stopping his nostrils with his hand.

God, however, was beginning to work in his life and causing him to do many things that startled him. One day as he was returning to Assisi and came close to the leper hospital at San Salvatore, to his horror he saw a leper standing in his path. The old loathing choked him but this time something, or *someone*, moved him to jump off his horse. He gave money to the leper and then gently took the hand and kissed it, putting his lips to the rotting flesh.

At that moment Francis saw the suffering Jesus in this suffering man. He put his arms around the leper. Francis' fear was gone. He mounted his horse again and continued on to Assisi with joy in his heart.[2]

In our own generation Mother Teresa in her phenomenal mission work among "the poorest of the poor" in the slums of Calcutta, India, had a similar approach. She habitually used the haunting phrase "his distressing disguise" to describe Jesus' presence among the poor, neglected people she met.

Henri Nouwen comments on the first time he met Douglas Steere, the Quaker retreat leader and author who has helped so many people deepen the inner life of the spirit. E. Glenn Hinson in his biography of Steere describes the scene: "Nouwen had invited him in April 1975 to Yale to speak to a class on spirituality. When he arrived at the train station in New Haven just after the passengers had disembarked, he looked down the platform to see this slightly stooped elderly gentleman in a charcoal suit lugging two heavy suitcases — not his own but those of another passenger who was having trouble carrying them."[3]

That was Douglas Steere. He could not only give a stimulating lecture but he knew most important of all what it was to put his faith into action wherever the occasion called for it. Those of us who have met him and have sat under his teaching that always stretched our minds also understood there was more to the man than his superb intellect. He was indeed a man who "walked the talk" and was constantly affirming and encouraging others.

Philip Yancey recalls one summer visiting a group of Wycliffe Bible Translators at their austere headquarters in the Arizona desert. They lived in mobile homes and their headquarters was a concrete-building with a metal roof.

However, Yancey was impressed by the personal dedication of these professional linguists who were preparing for a life of hardship in remote outposts in the world. They had a sense that serving God would make it worth their while, if not in this life then in the life to come.

While spending this time speaking to these highly trained but poorly paid Bible translators, Yancey would spend his early morning hours jogging along dirt roads in this desolate area. One morning he came upon a luxurious complex that included two Olympic swimming pools, aerobic workout rooms, lush gardens, even a baseball diamond and soccer fields. He learned that this imposing set of buildings belonged to a famous eating disorder clinic that caters to movie stars and athletes. Like the Wycliffe Bible Translators the staff was highly trained with a number of Ph.D.s and M.D.s but the clients who attended this clinic were charged $300 per day.

As Yancey jogged back to the humble mission base he was deeply conscious of the contrast between that and the spectacular eating disorder clinic. The one institution was preparing people to serve God and the other was preparing people to pamper their bodies and enjoy life without much thought of sacrifice. Yancey has interviewed many celebrities in his life and also unknown mission workers. The ones who seem to have the most satisfaction out of life are the latter who have caught something of the vision articulated in this parable. The world may value cure of the body more than cure of souls, but Yancey was convinced that the Wycliffe Bible Translators had something special that the other group did not have.[4]

The musical *Godspell* continues to inspire those who see it. We all have our favorite scenes in the musical. One of the most engaging scenes in my estimation is an episode in the Upper Room. Jesus takes a bucket of water, a cloth, and a mirror and he goes to each disciple. He washes away their painted clown faces. Then he holds up the mirror in front of their faces so that they can see themselves as they really are. Finally, he hugs each one.

It is not necessary for us to wear a false face, to pretend we are someone we are not. God loves us as we are. God accepts us with all our imperfections. Is not this teaching at the heart of the parable we are presently examining?

As usual, Eugene Peterson in *The Message*, expresses clearly and simply what Jesus means: "Whenever you did one of these things to someone overlooked or ignored, that was me — you did it to me."[5] Amen.

------

1. Leonard Sweet, *Out of the Question, Into the Mystery* (Colorado Springs, Colorado: Waterback Press, a division of Random House, Inc., 2004), 133.

2. Elizabeth Goudge, *My God and My All: The Life of Francis of Assisi* (New York: Coward-McCann, Inc., 1959), 36.

3. E. Glenn Hinson, *Love at the Heart of Things: A Biography of Douglas V. Steere* (Nashville: The Upper Room Books, 1998), xii.

4. Philip Yancey, *The Jesus I Never Knew* (Grand Rapids: Zondervan Publishing House, 1995), 110-111.

5. Eugene Peterson, *The Message: The Bible in Contemporary Language* (Colorado Springs, Colorado: Nav Press, 2002), 1797.

Epiphany of Our Lord
Matthew 2:1-12

Seeking the
Bethlehem Star

The Moravians, a small but influential Christian denomination, have a distinctive symbol known throughout the world. It is a large many-pointed star. This unusual star found in many Moravian homes is carefully preserved from year to year. As the Advent season approaches the star is brought out and hung in the hall or on the porch until the Festival of Epiphany, January 6.

This cherished Moravian star reminds the faithful of the star that led the wise men from their home in the distant East to Bethlehem where they presented gifts to the Christ Child.

When we examine the biblical story recorded in Matthew 2:1-12 about the original Bethlehem star a number of questions arise. One of the questions is: Can we identify the star that led the wise men to Bethlehem? We do not want for scientific explanations. Some say there was a conjunction of the planets Jupiter and Saturn. Others say the star was the spectacular Halley's Comet. Still others argue that it might have been a nova, an exploding star. All of these theories, while intriguing, are not foolproof.

Some biblical scholars see the Matthew birth narrative as a poetic or imaginative account to convey the important gospel message that God made himself present in the Messiah. Other believing Christians are content to accept the Bethlehem star as a supernatural event, not necessarily connected to any specific scientific explanation.

A second question that invariably arises is the identity of the wise men. Who were these men who had traveled from afar? The Greek word for the wise men is "magi." They probably were astrologers from Persia (modern-day Iran) who had a habit of exploring the skies. There is no hint in the text that they were kings as some of our Christmas carols imply. Nor can we be certain that there were three of them. The fact that three gifts are mentioned might suggest that number. Of course, the names later attached to them by tradition — Caspar, Melchior, and Balthasar — are entirely fictitious.

Finally, there is the question of the age of Jesus when the wise men appeared in Bethlehem. If we are to believe the numerous manger scenes at Christmas time, the shepherds and the wise men were present at the same time. Almost all biblical scholars, however, agree that the wise men came later, possibly a year or two after the birth of Jesus. Matthew 2:11 reads, "On entering the *house*, they saw the child with Mary his mother…" (Matthew 2:11). Apparently by the time the wise men arrived on the scene the holy family was living in a house and not in a more primitive manger setting.

What was the reaction to the birth of Jesus that is exhibited in Matthew's telling of the story? We see both negative and positive reactions. The negative reactions were displayed by King Herod, the chief priests, and scribes. King Herod was scared when he heard about a pretender to the throne being born. The last thing Herod wanted was the prospect of a new king challenging his throne. He was determined to stamp out the usurper before he could get started. The chief priests and scribes had a negative reaction too but it took more the form of a lack of interest. It is true they helped King Herod by telling him that according to the prophet Micah the Messiah was to be born in Bethlehem, but they didn't get too excited about the whole affair.

The positive reaction is seen in the attitude and actions of the wise men. According to Matthew, "On entering the house, they saw the child with Mary his mother; and they knelt down and paid him homage. Then, opening their treasure-chests, they offered him gifts of gold, frankincense, and myrrh" (Matthew 2:11). All these gifts were fit for a king. If we could find one word that would describe the wise men's positive reaction it would be "adoration."

A little boy did not say his prayers one night before going to bed. When asked why he did not pray, he replied candidly, "I didn't want anything last night."

Adoration is the opposite of this "gimme" prayer. Someone has said that adoring God is simply saying, "God, I love you." To adore is not to ask God for anything but to simply adore God as God, to love God as God.

Brant D. Baker in his provocative book, *Teaching P.R.A.Y.E.R.: Guidance for Pastors and Church Leaders*, has a chapter on adoration. He uses the insights of Chester Michael and Marie Norrisey to show how different personality types express their adoration in different ways. Being the good Catholics that they are, they have chosen four prominent church fathers to demonstrate four distinct types: Thomistic, Ignatian, Augustinian, and Franciscan.

Those who have the characteristics of Thomas Aquinas tend to be logical and rational in their prayer life. People with this temperament might want to study adoration from every possible angle asking a series of probing questions to get at the real heart of adoration.

Those who have the characteristics of Ignatius of Loyola, the founder of the Jesuit order, tend to enjoy ceremony and ritual. In particular they seek to use all five senses in imagining themselves in a particular scriptural story. For example, they imagine themselves to be Mary as she receives her guests, the wise men. What does she say? How does she feel?

People who have the characteristics of Augustine tend to be verbal, outspoken, and have a desire to discover what meaning in a given scriptural passage speaks to them. They also are apt to keep a spiritual journal of thoughts and inspirations that they record for future praise and adoration.

Those people who have the characteristics of Francis of Assisi tend to be free, unconfined, and impulsive. They prefer action and live very much in the present. Their adoration often sees God in the whole creation. Also, they like to use music, art, or dancing to express their praise of God.[1]

This is a helpful exercise for us to understand. While everyone should express adoration to God, it is possible to do so in a rich, variety of ways according to our individual temperaments.

The Psalms contain many prayers of adoration. Psalm 148 is a prime example. In verses 1-6 the psalmist calls upon the *heavens* to praise the Lord, that is, the angels, the sun, the moon, the shining stars, even the waters above the heavens are to praise God. Everything in the heavens is called upon to praise the Lord, their Creator.

In verses 7-14, the remainder of the psalm, the *earth* is called upon to praise the Lord, all sea monsters, fire and hail, snow and frost, strong winds, mountains and hills, fruit trees, wild animals, cattle, creeping things and flying birds, kings and princes, ordinary people, young men and women, and older people. In a word, everything on earth is to praise the Lord, with special recognition of the people of Israel, God's chosen people.

The prophets also expressed adoration.

> Jeremiah exclaimed: "There is none like you, O Lord; you are great, and your name is great in might. Who would not fear you, O King of the nations? For that is your due; among all the wise ones of the nations and in all their kingdoms there is no one like you."
> — Jeremiah 10:6-7

John Muir was born in Scotland. In 1849 his family moved to Wisconsin. He attended the University of Wisconsin but he did not graduate. He only took courses that interested him. Botany fascinated him. Soon Muir felt called to experience the world of nature firsthand. He walked 1,000 miles from the heartland of the country to the coast of Florida. This was just a tune up. He faced westward and walked all the way to California where he explored the gorgeous Yosemite Valley as no one had done before him. Still later, he explored the magnificent Alaskan glaciers. He was always on the move and no one was thrilled more than he was simply to be in the wilderness that God had created.

One of my favorite stories from Muir's journals happened in December 1874 when he took a trip into the Sierra Mountains of California and he was caught in a violent windstorm. Instead of camping he decided to climb to the top of a tree to see what it would feel like in the center of the windstorm. He selected one of the tallest of the Douglas Spruce trees, over 100 feet high. He climbed to the top of the tree, and he said, "... never before did I enjoy so noble an exhilaration of motion." He clung to the tree with muscles firmly braced as the slender top flapped and swished in the passionate torment of the driving wind. He estimated the sweeps of his treetop described an arc of from twenty to thirty degrees.

"I kept my lofty perch for hours," he wrote, "frequently closing my eyes to enjoy the music by itself, or to feast quietly on the delicious fragrance that was streaming past." When the storm began to abate, Muir dismounted and sauntered through the calming woods.[2]

What Muir teaches me about God's creation is that it is to be experienced to the hilt. Perhaps we will not climb a tall tree in a violent windstorm like he did, but adoring God by walking in the splendor of the great outdoors is surely one way of expressing praise to God. God is not nature, and nature is not God. To think that way would be to think like a pantheist and not like a person of biblical faith. But God is *in* nature. God comes through it like electricity through a wire. The wire is not electricity, but it can be a vehicle through which the electricity flows.

With the prophet Jeremiah, we all can shout, "There is no one like you, O Lord; you are great..." (Jeremiah 10:6).

In other words, the prayer of adoration does not praise God because we have received help or our prayers are answered. We love God simply because God is God. We are happy to be in God's presence with a sense of awe and reverence. Adoration intensifies our relationship with God and reminds us that God is not to serve us but we are to serve God.

Best-selling author Philip Yancey lives in the mountains of Colorado. He is a mountain-climber who thrills in attempting to climb the 14,000 foot peaks around his home. From the vantage point of the summit he realizes how small he is and he gets a fractional glimpse of what God must see all the time.

In Yancey's entrancing book, *Prayer: Does It Make Any Difference?*, he recalls a passage from Thorton Wilder's play, "Our Town." Jane, one of the characters in the play, gets a letter addressed to her farm, town, county, state, and the envelope continues, "The United States of America; Continent of North America; Western Hemisphere; the Earth; the Solar System; the Universe; the Mind of God."

Yancey asks if not it would be best if we reversed the order and began with the mind of God. If we did this, perhaps the rest of our lives would fall into place. Yancey concludes by stating, "It occurs to me, thinking about prayer, that most of the time I get the direction wrong. I start downstream with my own concerns and bring them to God... Instead, I should start upstream where the flow begins."[3]

Adoration, as the wise men knew long ago, is an essential beginning for genuine prayer, in fact, for life itself. Amen.

1. Brant D. Baker, *Teaching P.R.A.Y.E.R.: Guidance for Pastors and Church Leaders* (Nashville: Abingdon Press, 2001), 105-109.

2. *The Wilderness World of John Muir* with an Introduction and Interpretive Comments by Edwin Way Teale (Boston: Houghton Mifflin Company, 1954), 186-190.

3. Philip Yancey, *Prayer: Does It Make Any Difference?* (Grand Rapids: Zondervan, 2006), 23.

Baptism of Our Lord
Epiphany 1
Ordinary Time 1
Mark 1:4-11

Baptizing in the Spirit

In Alex Haley's pioneer study, *Roots*, there is a poignant scene when Kunta Kinta, a slave, drives his master to a ball at a nearby plantation house. He parks his buggy and resigns himself to a long wait until it is time to take his master home again. At first, he listens to the white man's music emanating from the plantation house. Then he begins to hear in the distance other music with a different rhythm. He follows the sound down a path behind the house leading to a few humble cabins. What he hears is African music, melodies that he recalls from his early childhood.

Kunta meets a man who is from the same section of Africa where he had once lived. They are deliriously happy as they talk in their native language about those early days. That night Kunta lay weeping as he couldn't sleep. The African music had helped him to remember who he was.[1]

Baptism gives us a sense of identity and tells us who we are. In addition, baptism gives us a sense of function and tells us what we are to do.

Mark summarizes the baptism of Jesus in a brief paragraph.

> In those days Jesus came from Nazareth of Galilee and was baptized by John in the Jordan. And just as he was coming up out of the water, he saw the heavens torn apart and the Spirit descending like a dove on him. And a voice came from heaven, "You are my Son, the Beloved; with you I am well pleased."
>
> — Mark 1:9-11

We have already described John the Baptist, his person and his message, in two of our earlier Advent sermons; now our focus is upon Jesus and his baptism.

The words that Jesus heard at his baptism gave him a sense of *identity*: "You are my Son, the Beloved; with you I am well pleased." He knew who he was. Jesus made it clear in his teaching and ministry that the same voice he heard at the Jordan River may be heard among his followers today. In their baptism they too hear that God accepts them and will care for them from the beginning of their journey to the end.

When Jesus first approached John to be baptized just like the other people were being baptized by John, the wilderness prophet was reluctant to do so. He did not think it was necessary for Jesus to undergo baptism, but Jesus insisted that he be baptized so that he could completely identify with his people, Israel. Matthew in his gospel has Jesus saying: "Let it be so now; for it is proper for us in this way to fulfill all righteousness" (Matthew 3:15).

These words of Jesus have puzzled Christians through the centuries. What could they possibly mean? "Righteousness" usually means doing the will of God. To "fulfill" all righteousness meant doing or performing the will of God. Notice that becoming part of God's redemptive plan was something Jesus and John should do together.

Fred and Sue Ann Schmidt, ministers of the gospel, have begun to build a retirement home. In a recent sermon Sue Ann explained how they are going about the construction of the house. They are actually building a "house around a house." Fred grew up on a farm on the edge of the Amish country in Ohio. He recalls his father building the house with the help of his firemen buddies and Amish friends. His father took down an abandoned church building and used the wonderful walnut beams and lumber incorporating them in a tiny brick house for his wife and son on a sixty-acre farm. In the years since Fred's parents have died, a number of people have rented the house. It has always been a dream of Fred's that when he retired he would return to the farm and to this house that his father had built in the 1940s.

The time has arrived for retirement. Fred and Sue Ann realized that they would need a bit more house now that they have seven children and sixteen grandchildren. Therefore, they found an Amish man and his five sons to build the new structure.

The foundation of the existing house was solid. Fred's father had used the firm soil and all the thousands of sandstone rocks found in that area which provided a solid base. Now the builders raised the roof to accommodate new rooms, rebuilt the chimney over the roofline, and excavated enough ground to lay a foundation for the add-on part. Some contractors might have wanted to take down the old structure and simply start over, but this builder was more than willing to use what was there, maintaining the integrity of the memories Fred has of his father's hard work and precision building. Like Jesus in his desire to relate to the past of Israel's tradition, as he began a new ministry, even so Fred and Sue Ann did not want to forget Fred's heritage at the same time moving ahead into the new adventure of retirement.[2]

"What's in a name?" Shakespeare asked the question and went on to say, "A rose by any other name would smell just as sweet." Maybe a name does not really matter. As children we probably once chanted, "Sticks and bones can break my bones but names can never hurt me."

But names can hurt. If we are considered a problem child or a cantankerous adult, it hurts. If we are called ugly or stupid, it hurts. Parents, teachers, and other authority figures sometimes tell us we need to prove ourselves and then we will be loved and accepted.

Rather than setting forth this negative message, baptism is more affirming saying that in God's sight we are "Beloved."

We all fail miserably at times, even Henri Nouwen who has helped so many people on their spiritual journey fails but he is reminded: "… the Father is always looking for me with outstretched arms to receive me back and whisper again in my ear: 'You are my Beloved, on you my favor rests.' "[3]

Whether young or old each one is baptized in the name of Jesus Christ, and that is why baptism is sometimes referred to as "Christening." Whatever our name may be, in baptism we are set apart in the name of Christ as one of his followers. We have a specific identity. We are special people. God says to us, "You are my Beloved, with you I am well pleased."

Martin Luther, the great German reformer of the sixteenth century, to whom we all are indebted, usually is remembered as a man of remarkable faith, and rightly so. His key words of "justification by faith" found in the apostle Paul's writings, not only changed his own life but became the watchword of the Reformation. He was a man of courage who challenged the oppressive powers of the church and the state. Luther also had his moments of doubt; indeed he suffered long bouts of depression (*anfechtung*). When he felt himself threatened he would pull himself out of the tailspin by saying to himself, "I am baptized. I am baptized." That affirmation brought to mind that God's love had marked him long ago and would never desert him.[4]

Baptism not only gives us an identity but also an awareness of our *function*. We know not just who we are but also what we are called to do. At Jesus' baptism he not only had the assurance of God's approval, but "he also saw the heavens torn apart and the Spirit descending like a dove on him" — in a word he received power to exercise his ministry.

As followers of Jesus we all need this same power to discharge our own ministries. Sometimes we need a little extra. I heard of a pastor about to baptize a baby turning to the father and asking the name of the child. The father replied, "Justin Winthrop Charles Adam Lucius McWilliams." The pastor turned to his associate and said, "A little more water, please."[5]

Although we have many different jobs, as Christians we have one essential calling — to serve in Jesus' name. We share the good news and above all we live the good news. As we serve in Jesus' name we take chances and risks, and we may even have to suffer as Jesus did. It can be a costly adventure.

Not only as individual disciples but as a whole congregation we are poised at the beginning of the new year to see where real needs are. We want to bring God's love to anyone who is hurting. It may be a sacrificial endeavor but it will be worth every ounce of effort we put into it.

Of course, we cannot fulfill our function, obvious as it may be, in our own strength and power. Even though Jesus became fully aware of his acceptance by the Father, yet he also needed the motivating power of the Holy Spirit to accomplish the work he was called to do. Likewise, God gives us the same Spirit to do the tasks we are summoned to do.

In the early Christian church of the first few centuries, the new members admitted by the sign of baptism were impressed with the seriousness of their commitment and an understanding that they were not only accepted unconditionally by God's love but they also had a function to perform as disciples of Jesus. All were baptized according to the Trinitarian formula that concludes the gospel of Matthew: "in the name of the Father and of the Son and of the Holy Spirit" (Matthew 28:19).

The candidates of baptism received intense instruction in the faith, in some cases the instruction lasted three years. The candidates (catechumens) were permitted to worship during their preparation, at least for part of the service. They were required to leave before the Communion service when the Eucharist was celebrated.

Baptism was usually by immersion in water. In some churches the candidates were baptized naked, the children first, then the men, and at the last the women. Also, in the early church the laying on of hands followed the baptism symbolizing the reception of the Holy Spirit. Easter or the fifty days after Easter became the most prominent time for the baptism ceremony.

Everything was done in getting the candidates ready for baptism to underscore their personal responsibility in responding to God's grace. They were asked to take vows that included renunciation and affirmation. Later, when children were baptized the parents and sponsors took the same vows on behalf of the children. The vows might include questions like the following:

> Do you renounce evil and its power in the world,
> which defies God's righteousness and love?
> Reply: I renounce them.
> Do you renounce the way of sin that separates you
> from the love of God?
> Reply: I renounce them.
> Do you turn to Jesus Christ and accept him as your
> Lord and Savior?
> Reply: I do.
> Do you intend to be Christ's faithful disciple, obeying
> his word and showing his love, to your life's end?
> Reply: I do.

Today in many churches words similar to these are being used to accent the function of the new member of the church as being a faithful Christian disciple prepared to serve others.

Native Americans used to have a unique practice for training young braves. When a boy turned thirteen, and after learning the skills of hunting, scouting, and fishing, he was blindfolded and taken several miles away. When he took off his blindfold, he was in the middle of a deep, dark forest where he had to spend the entire night alone.

You can imagine how the young brave felt. Every time he heard a twig snap he could imagine a wild animal ready to pounce upon him. Every time the wind blew he wondered what sinister sound it masked. It would be a long, long night for the young boy being initiated.

After what seemed like forever, the dawn came. Looking around the boy saw flowers, trees, and a path out of the woods. Then, to his astonishment, he saw a man standing just a few feet away armed with a bow and arrow.

It was the boy's father. He had been there throughout the night. What a way to teach a young boy how God allows us to face the challenges of life. God is always present with us. God's Spirit, the same Spirit that came to Jesus in his baptism, comes to us in our baptism and protects us, directs us, empowers us to do what God has called us to do in our individual lives.[6]

There is nothing like being baptized in the Spirit! God is with us all the time, to the end of time.

> Christ be with me, Christ within me,
> Christ behind me, Christ before me,
> Christ beside me, Christ to win me,
> Christ to comfort and restore me,
> Christ beneath me, Christ above me,
> Christ in quiet, Christ in danger,
> Christ in hearts of all that love me,
> Christ in mouth of friend and stranger.
> — Saint Patrick's Breastplate

Amen.

---

1. Story quoted in William H. Willimon, *Remember Who You Are: Baptism, a Model for Christian Life* (Nashville: The Upper Room, 1980), 113.
2. From a sermon preached by the Rev. Sue Ann Schmidt at the First Congregational Church, Hudson, Ohio, February 20, 2011.

3. Henri J.M. Nouwen, *The Return of the Prodigal Son: A Story of Homecoming* (New York: Doubleday, Image Books, 1994), 44.

4. Roland Bainton, *Here I Stand: A Life of Martin Luther* (New York: A Mentor Book published by The New American Library, 1955), 287.

5. Leonard Sweet, *Soul Tsunami* (Grand Rapids: Zondervan Publishing House, 1999), 237.

6. Leonard Sweet, *Soul Salsa* (Grand Rapids: Zondervan Publishing House, 2000), 23-24.

Seeing Is Believing

Eugene Peterson tells about his boyhood days growing up in the "Big Sky" country of Montana. One day as a five-year-old Eugene stood at a barbed wire fence looking at a farmer plowing the field with his enormous tractor. The thing the boy wished for most in those days was to get a ride on a John Deere tractor. The boy knew the man driving the tractor was Brother Storm who always sat at the back of the church. Suddenly, the man stopped the tractor, stood up, and from his seat began to make strong waving motions with his arms. The big man looked mean and angry. He was a large and ominous man in his bib overalls and straw hat. The wind was blowing against him so the little boy couldn't make out his words, but he knew he was yelling at him. He probably should not be where he was on the fence. He decided he better get out of there fast.

The next Sunday after worship Brother Storm came over to the boy, and said, "Little Pete, why didn't you come out in the field Thursday and ride the tractor with me?" The stunned boy replied, "I didn't know I could have, I thought you were chasing me away." "No," the man replied, "I called you to come. I waved for you to come."[1]

It is easy to misinterpret what someone is trying to say to us, but there could be no misinterpreting Philip's call to Nathanael in our scripture today when he said simply, "Come and see."

Philip had met Jesus and he wanted his friend Nathanael to know him too. It was only when Philip told Nathanael that Jesus was from Nazareth that a stumbling block occurred.

Nathanael's hometown was Cana — only a few miles from Nazareth. As they say, familiarity breeds contempt, and Nathanael reasoned how can anything good come out of such a tiny village of Nazareth that he knew so well. Surely, if Jesus was the Messiah he would have come from Jerusalem, or at least from Bethlehem the smaller town mentioned by the prophet Micah. But Nazareth seemed impossible!

We don't know very much about Nathanael. He is not listed with the twelve in either Mark's or in Matthew's account of the twelve disciples. He does appear later in the gospel of John (21:2) where he is identified as one of the followers who met the risen Jesus by the sea of Tiberius. At one time it was thought that Nathanael might have had another name, Bartholomew, because he is mentioned in Mark's and Matthew's accounts of the twelve and his name appears right after Philip. But this theory is not held by many biblical scholars today.

In any event, Nathanael is hard to convince that Jesus is the Messiah until he meets Jesus who greets him with the words, "Here is truly an Israelite in whom there is no deceit!" (John 1:47). Nathanael is astonished that Jesus could say that about him without knowing him. He was further mystified when Jesus added, "I saw you under the fig tree before Philip called you" (John 1:48).

Did Jesus sense that Nathanael too was yearning for the Day of the Lord and the coming of the Messiah? Nathanael undoubtedly was aware that the prophet Micah had once written that faithful Israelites would one day "sit under their own vines and under their own fig tree and no one shall make them afraid": for the mouth of the Lord of hosts has spoken (Micah 4:4).

Jesus continued by saying that one day Nathanael would even "see heaven opened and the angels of God ascending and descending upon the Son of Man" (John 1:51). These last words are an obvious reference to the patriarch Jacob's experience of God at Bethel where he saw in a dream "angels ascending and descending." Unlike Nathanael, Jacob had been a deceitful person prior to the Bethel episode. If God had called Jacob to serve him, how much more was he apt to call Nathanael, "a man with no deceit"? In other words, one day Nathanael will see Jesus in his fullness as the Messiah and in his role as mediator between heaven and earth.

Philip gives us in capsule form a method of reaching out to others with the good news about Jesus. He plainly said, "Come and see." He didn't badger or belittle Nathanael because he did not know the Messiah had arrived. He didn't even attempt to argue with him or reason him into the kingdom of God. He said, "Come and see." It was as if he said, "Seeing is believing."

William Coffin, Chaplain at Yale University for eighteen years, often encountered much skepticism about God not just from young students but also from his colleagues — professors at the university. When some of these professors would mock religion in his presence he would invariably ask them, "Tell me about the God you don't believe in." Coffin knew that 99 chances out of a 100 he wouldn't believe in their kind of God either. Coffin habitually quoted one of his favorite philosophers, Blaise Pascal, who once wrote: "The heart has reasons of which the mind knows nothing."[2]

Attempting to assure someone that God exists or that they should consider following Jesus seldom works. Philip's "come and see" approach is a much better way.

A number of congregations I know have committees called "Come and See." The purpose of these committees is not to do the work of evangelism for the whole congregation but to motivate, inspire, and instruct the congregation to be a welcoming community of faith.

One congregation I know operates as follows. They have welcoming bags at the door for all first-time visitors. These bags contain information about the church including a DVD setting forth the congregation's varied mission programs including a ministry to the homeless, regular visits to the inner city to man food pantries, and to carry on other social justice programs.

This particular congregation not only invites visitors who attend worship to become part of their fellowship of faith but its members go out where the people are and listen to them, ascertain their perceived needs, and then share the good news. Their aim essentially is to seek a commitment not to an institution but to a person, a commitment to Jesus Christ.

We may perceive ourselves to be a "welcoming" church, but others may discern us differently. They may not know how to get in.

Vincent van Gogh, the great Dutch artist, had been a lay preacher to coal miners in his early adult years, but he became troubled in spirit at the lack of success of his art career. It was only after his death that his art was really appreciated. Today his paintings sell in the millions. A few weeks before van Gogh took his own life he painted a picture of a church known as "The Church at Auvers." As you look at the church in the picture, it emanates a dimly eerie light from the inside, but you look more closely and notice that the church has no doors. There is no way to get in.

How haunting! How many others around us today can't find a way in?

Of course, we may have the dogmatic attitude that we don't want too many people in our church if they are not the right kind of people. Lewis Smedes tells of such congregations he once knew: "When I was a parish minister, I came across a group of three Dutch families in Paterson, New Jersey, who had joined together to form what they believed to be the only true Christian church in America but they had a disagreement. Finding no way to resolve it, they split into two churches, one with two and other with one family, each sure that it was the only true Christian church in America."[3]

But the simple fact of the matter is that we do need each other. Our doors should be open wide to welcome everyone no matter where they might be on their journey.

Rabbi Harold S. Kushner tells the story of one day when he was at the beach he observed two children, a boy and a girl, playing in the sand. They were hard at work building a sand castle that had gates and towers and moats and internal passages. Just when they were nearly finished building the sand castle, a huge wave came along and knocked it down. Kushner said that he expected the children would burst into tears but they surprised him. Instead, they ran up the bank away from the shore, laughing and holding hands, and sat down to build another castle.

Kushner reflected upon what he saw: "I realized that they had taught me an important lesson. All the things in our lives, all the complicated structures we spend so much time and energy creating, are built on sand. Only our relationships with other people endure. Sooner or later, the wave will come along and knock down what we have worked so hard to build up. When that happens, only the person who has somebody's hand to hold will be able to laugh."[4]

Holding hands eases hurts, pain, and disappointment. We welcome "whosoever may come" into our fellowship. We need each other. We do not want to be a church of the "closed door."

If we have a compelling story to tell, and we do, we also need to be willing to listen to stories of other people who may see things differently from the way we do. We do not need to accept everything we hear but we need to listen. The Christian faith is not so much propositional as it is relational, and all relationships take time to cultivate. We do need to hold hands, to learn from one another, and to support one another.

Ann Lamott in her poignant memoir, *Traveling Mercies*, tells about responding to an invitation to visit a small, black congregation on the fringe of San Francisco. She went there time and time again with mixed feelings. The church was called St. Andrew Presbyterian, and it looked homely and impoverished, a ramshackle building with a small cross on top. Ann was mesmerized by the hymns wafting out of the church building and she would stop and listen. She would stop occasionally and stand in the doorway to listen to the songs. The choir consisted of five black women and one "rather Amish-looking white man" but together they made a glorious noise. The worshiping congregation consisted of about thirty people. Once in a while various people would come back to the door and shake hands with Ann or give her a hug. The pastor spoke mostly about Jesus and social injustice.

Ann went back to the church about once a month but usually left before the sermon. She didn't want to be preached to but she did love the people and the children who were always running around or being embraced. Every other week the people brought in huge tubs of food for the homeless families living in the nearby shelters. But it was singing above all else that captivated her. She would sing along even though she was still standing in the doorway.

Finally, one Sunday she decided to sit on one of the folding chairs off by herself. The singing continued to be breath and food for her. She had been drinking heavily and carousing and she became sick. As she lay in her bed one night she had the sensation of someone being with her, "hunkered down in the corner." At first, she thought it might be her father who had died recently, then she realized it was Jesus. She was appalled when she thought about her hilarious progressive friends. What would they think of her if she became a Christian? She turned to the wall and said out loud, "I would rather die."

Nonetheless, she felt him just sitting there on his haunches in the corner of her sleeping loft, watching her with patience and love. Finally, she fell asleep and in the morning he was gone. During the day she felt that a little cat was following her, wanting her to reach down, pick it up, open the door, and let it in. But she knew what would happen: You let a cat in one time, give it a little milk, and then it stays forever. So she tried to keep one step ahead of it, slamming her houseboat door when she entered and left.

The next week she went to church and she stayed for the sermon. Once again the sermon did not make sense to her but the last hymn caused her to weep and be filled with joy at the same time. Something was holding her and rocking her like a scared kid. She opened to that feeling and it washed over her.

Ann left the service before the benediction. She ran home and felt the little cat running along at her heels. She opened the door to her houseboat. Finally, she cried to herself, "… I quit," and said out loud, "All right, you can come in."[5]

This was how she described her moment of conversion.

It took Ann a long time but eventually this welcoming congregation with its open invitation of "come and see" set her on a remarkable journey of faith. Whether it is a short length of time or a longer time, the same thing can happen to us. Amen.

---

1. Eugene H. Peterson, *Under the Unpredictable Plant* (Grand Rapids: William B. Eerdmans Publishing Company, 1992), 158-160.

2. William Sloan Coffin, *Letters to a Young Doubter* (Louisville: Westminster John Knox Press, 2005), 3, 17-18.

3. Lewis Smedes, *My God and I* (Grand Rapids: Eerdmans Publishing Company, 2003), 92-93.

4. Quoted in Leonard Sweet, *A Cup of Coffee at Soul Café* (Nashville: Broadman & Holman Publishers, 1998), 29-30.

5. Ann Lamott, *Traveling Mercies: Some Thoughts on Faith* (New York: Anchor Books, a Division of Random Harvest, Inc., 1999), 50.

Proclaiming the Good News

In Washington Irving's *Sketch Book* he tells of a whimsical character by the name of Rip Van Winkle. This man will be remembered as long as American literature lives. According to the story he went to sleep for twenty years during the late Colonial period. When he awoke a new nation had been born and George Washington was president.

Rip Van Winkle had slept through a revolution.

Likewise, the four fishermen mentioned in Mark's gospel: Peter, Andrew, James, and John. They heard Jesus' revolutionary words and they were called to enter a new era, a new adventure that they never could have dreamed of before this call came.

As usual Mark is brief and to the point. He sums up Jesus' proclamation of the good news in this manner: "The time is fulfilled, and the kingdom of God has come near; repent, and believe in the good news" (Mark 1:15). Then Jesus walks along the Sea of Galilee and calls individual fishermen to follow him. Each one "immediately" left what they were doing and followed him. One of Mark's favorite words is "immediately." He uses this word no less than 41 times in his gospel.

We might say at this point that reading the other gospels we get the impression this probably was not the first time that these four men met Jesus. They had had previous contact and now they were being called to definite service in following Jesus.

Mark does not give us much description regarding this scene. We do not know whether these fishermen really enjoyed their work or not. We do know how they related to each other. We do not know what kind of day it was. Was the sun shining or was it a cloudy day?

Mark refers to the Sea of Galilee. We know that this "sea" was actually a "lake" about thirteen miles long and six miles at its widest lying 682 feet below sea level. Luke who knew something about the terrors of the real sea, in his gospel, called this body of water a "lake."

Despite the scarcity of details we cannot underestimate the call of Jesus and the response of these men to become disciples. We have the beginning of a new community of faith. Albert Schweitzer, the missionary doctor, theologian, and Bach specialist, in his book, *The Quest of the Historical Jesus*, has written these oft-quoted words:

> He comes to us as One unknown, without a name, as of old, by the lakeside. He came to those men who knew Him not. He speaks to us the same word: "Follow thou me!" and sets us to the tasks which He has to fulfill for our time. He commands. And to those who obey Him, whether they be wise or simple, He will reveal Himself in the toils, the conflicts, the sufferings that they shall pass through in His fellowship, and as an ineffable mystery, they shall learn in their own experience Who He is.[1]

Although each of the four disciples mentioned in this passage are important I am going to focus primarily on Andrew because he is customarily relegated to a minor role in contrast to the other three who formed Jesus' inner circle of intimate disciples.

Even though Andrew does not stand out in quite the same way that Peter, James, and John do in our memory of the twelve, Andrew has become the patron saint of no less than three nations. Russia is one of these nations. Tradition says that Andrew in his mission work traveled into the region north of the Black Sea, what is now modern-day Russia.

Tradition also says that Andrew died a martyr's death in Greece. According to historians Andrew was crucified on a cross like Jesus, but he insisted that he was unworthy to die on the same kind of cross and asked to be crucified on a X-shaped cross, to this day known as the Saint Andrew's cross.

Finally, tradition tells us that Andrew is associated with Scotland. A monk by the name of Regulus took some of the relics of Andrew with him as he did mission work on the east coast of Scotland at the place where the town of St. Andrews is today.

Of course, some people think St. Andrews is the most sacred place on earth because it is the birthplace of the game of golf.

I once had a friend who loved to play golf; in fact, he was fanatical about the game. One day he came to me and said, "My wife has given me an ultimatum. She said, 'It is either golf or me.' He confided in me, 'I am sure going to miss my wife.' " He was only kidding, I hope.

Although Andrew is named "St. Andrew" in some quarters today, we must not think of him as a plaster saint. He was a real human being, rather ordinary, a real flesh and blood person like we are. He was more of a utility player than a superstar on Jesus' team. He tended to stay in the background. But think about this: He is only mentioned three times in the gospel of John and each time he is mentioned he is bringing someone to see Jesus.

First of all, Andrew brings Peter to Jesus.

As the gospel of John opens in the very first chapter we learn that Andrew and Philip are disciples of John the Baptist, but one day John startles them by pointing to a stranger who appeared on the scene. John cried out, "Behold, the Lamb of God." From that time on Andrew and Philip left John the Baptist and began to follow Jesus.

Furthermore, Andrew was so excited about this new relationship that he went home to find his brother, Simon (later called Peter) and said to him, "We have found the Messiah (which means Christ). He brought him to Jesus."

Andrew is to be commended for proclaiming the good news about Jesus, and he is doubly commended because in introducing his brother to Jesus he knew that he himself would be over-shadowed. Peter was the "loud mouth" in the family. Every time Andrew wanted to say a word Peter beat him to it. Andrew knew that if he told Jesus about his brother he would have to play "second fiddle" in the disciple's band.

If you observe the references to Andrew in the gospel of Mark and the gospel of John, in fact in all four gospels, almost every time Andrew is mentioned he is identified as "Andrew, Simon Peter's brother." It is almost as if the gospel writers are trying to remember who this guy is. "Who was Andrew?" Oh, yes, now I remember, he was "Simon Peter's brother." I better make a note of that connection and then I will remember him.

Knowing all this, to Andrew's credit he was willing to stay in the background because he knew how much Jesus could do for his brother, and he also knew that Peter could make a special contribution among Jesus' disciples. As we know, Peter eventually became the leader and spokesman for the twelve disciples.

Spring training at the major league baseball camps in Florida and in Arizona will soon be here. The pitchers and catchers will be the first to arrive then the rest of the team will follow in a week or two. The star players, of course, will garner the headlines. But I have observed that managers and coaches even at this early date are looking for a few good utility players to play the infield or the outfield. The managers and coaches know that many star players are prone to injuries. It is a long season, and if they do not have players they can insert in the game when injuries occur or when the regular players are tired near the end of the season, they are apt to be a struggling team. The utility player is usually versatile and can play a variety of positions as needed. He may go up to the plate and not swing for the fences but he knows how to lay down a good bunt and occasionally he slashes an extra base hit at the opportune time. On the whole, he is kept ready because he is a good defensive player who often makes a play that saves the game.

How we need "utility players" like Andrew in the church today! They are willing to stay in the background until the time arrives to do something significant. They also are not hesitant to bring others into the fellowship of faith, new disciples who might in the end outshine them.

The next time Andrew is mentioned in the gospel of John he is bringing a young lad to Jesus.

The scene is a familiar one to many of us. Jesus has been speaking to a crowd, estimated to be 5,000 men. But near the close of day when it was time to go home, the crowd remained past the supper hour. Philip became alarmed and began to complain. Philip often sensed the need of people but he never seemed to know what to do about it.

Andrew, on the other hand, not only sensed the seriousness of the situation but he sought a means to alleviate the crisis. Looking around the crowd, Andrew found a lad who had brought a few provisions with him. He took the boy to Jesus.

Andrew said to Jesus, "There is a boy here who has five barley loaves and two fish. But what are they among so many people?" Those last words probably indicate that Andrew was not sure that such meager provisions would meet the needs of the whole crowd. The important thing is that he brought what he could find to Jesus. As we know, but do not understand exactly how, Jesus took these few provisions and in some manner, fed the whole crowd.[2]

Itzhak Perlman, one of the greatest violinists of all time played at Lincoln Center in New York City in 1995. Perlman, afflicted by polio since he was a child, walked on stage with heavy braces on both legs. He also needed crutches in order to walk. On this occasion as he was playing, suddenly there was a loud noise, one of the strings on his violin broke. Most people thought Perlman would leave the stage and get another violin.

Instead, he sat there for a few moments, closed his eyes, and asked the conductor to begin again. He played the entire piece with great passion on just three strings. You can imagine the applause when Perlman concluded his performance. When the cheering stopped, Perlman explained: "Sometimes it is the artist's task to find out how much music you can still make with what you have left."[3]

Time and time again we think our resources are too small to accomplish anything significant, but when we bring what we have to Jesus he has a way of multiplying what we bring into something greater than we could ever dream could happen.

The third and last time Andrew is mentioned in the gospel of John he is still bringing people to Jesus. This time it is a group of people, simply described as "some Greeks."

The setting is the Passover feast in Jerusalem shortly before Jesus' death upon the cross. Faithful Jews have come from all over the world to be present at the feast. These men first of all approached Philip and asked him, "Sir, we would see Jesus." Philip once again is not quite sure what he should do; therefore, as before, he goes to Andrew. Perhaps Philip wasn't even sure the foreigners were Jews. Andrew didn't care about their religious affiliation and so he took them to see Jesus.

Jesus did speak to them saying something about a grain falling in the earth, dying, and producing much fruit. Could this have been an allusion to the fact that one day the good news would be proclaimed beyond the tiny boundaries of Palestine and would reach the Gentiles? Could the men standing before Jesus be "the first fruits" of that great harvest?[4]

I have heard of a contemporary church that calls their outreach committee "Operation Andrew." After reviewing Andrew's life we can see why they might use his name. In some ways, Andrew might be considered the founder of "local missions" because he brought his brother Peter to Jesus. Also, he might be regarded as the founder of "world missions" because he brought the Greeks, representatives of the larger world, to Jesus.

Most congregations today are actively involved in both home and world missions. Is it possible that we have missed a crucial mission field? I wonder where Andrew, who responded to Jesus' call to "fish for people," would see our greatest opportunity for mission today. Where are the multitudes at this present time?

Let me close by reading a letter sent to a pastor in Hilliard, Ohio, not far from Columbus. A young woman of the congregation wrote this letter to her pastor. I will quote it verbatim.

Dear Max,

Last night I had an interesting experience that I would like to share with you. I sometimes venture among strangers to see how Jesus is working in the world. I was at a place with lots of rooms — people gathering for all kinds of purposes. One sign said, "Christian Fellowship" so that's where I went.

The room was nearly packed and a lot of conversation going on. I was drawn to a group where one young woman was really struggling. She was raised by, and lives with a family of Satanists (unbelievable) but some how, Christ must have touched her because she was trying to find her way into the light. Since I was a latecomer, I didn't know her background — but a few people were talking to her and trying to help her. I'm usually too private about my faith (you know, don't wear that button out into the world).

... The love and presence of Jesus in that room was awesome. We held hands, cried, prayed, gave thanks... eventually we were led in prayer and this girl and one other turned their lives over to God....

There are more details to this story, but they aren't important to share at the moment. What I do want to share though is why I am writing to you. I just wanted to let you know that **Jesus is alive in cyberspace**. Thought that you could appreciate that. Yes, what I am saying is that all this took place by way of my computer.

If you are interested and the Spirit moves you, I am open to further discussion. Do you suppose that one day the church might support mission work out there in cyberspace? There are certainly a lot of lost, searching souls there.

In Jesus' name.

Betsy[5]

Where are the multitudes today? They are inside their electronic cottages plugged into a variety of media outlets. Is one of our major mission fields today to the take the good news about Jesus to meet people where they are — staring at their screens in their homes? Amen.

---

1. Quoted in Lamar Williamson Jr., *Interpretation, A Bible Commentary for Teaching and Preaching* (Louisville: John Knox Press, 1983), 48.
2. William Barclay, *The Gospel of John*, Volume 1 (Philadelphia: The Westminster Press, 1955), 73-74, 204.
3. James W. Moore, *If God Has a Refrigerator, Your Picture Is On It* (Nashville: Dimensions for Living, 2003), 65-66.
4. William Barclay, *The Gospel of John*, Volume 2 (Louisville: Westminster John Knox, 1974), 139-140.
5. Leonard Sweet, *The Jesus Prescription for a Healthy Life* (Nashville: Abingdon Press, 1996), 80-81.

Recognizing the Voice of Authority

This story may be apocryphal, but I heard of a professor who was not only popular on campus but also was in demand in Washington DC to help out with governmental matters. Occasionally, he was called away from his academic environment to spend time consulting in Washington DC. One time when he left for two weeks he told his class that they had important work to finish so while he was away they should come to class and he would have all his lectures taped for them.

The professor went away and as it so happened during the two-week period he had to travel near the university. He thought he would stop by and see how things were going in his class. Sure enough, as he approached the classroom he could hear his own voice on tape giving the lecture. But when he opened the door no students were present. Instead, he observed at each desk was a tape recorder taking down the professor's notes.

Sometimes when we think we have everything under control, events turn out differently from what we had planned.

Jesus was a rabbi or teacher. In this first chapter in the gospel of Mark, Jesus is teaching in the synagogue in Capernaum. The people are astounded at his teaching, which is different from the teaching of the scribes. The scribes, most of whom, belong to the sect of the Pharisees, rely on the teachings of the Torah, the Law of Moses, but also rely on the teachings of the oral tradition that has accumulated through the centuries. Therefore, they buttress their arguments with a variety of interpretations, and sometimes they are a bit confusing on certain issues. They were inclined to say rabbi #1 says this, and rabbi #2 says that and as a result, the people were not always certain what was the correct interpretation. But Jesus is distinctive in that "he taught them as one having authority" (Mark 1:22). We know nothing about the details of Jesus' teaching that day except that the quality was new and refreshing. He did not quote other authorities; he spoke authoritatively himself as if he knew what he was talking about with little ambiguity. It was almost like he believed he had been "assigned" to speak on behalf of God.

Suddenly the synagogue service is interrupted by the appearance of "a man with an unclean spirit." An unclean spirit meant the man was possessed of a demon. It was commonly believed in Jesus' day that some people were overcome with the power of evil to such an extent that they could not control themselves. These people tended to live in "unclean" places in the mountains or in the desert away from the mainstream of society. From our vantage point in the twenty-first century it is difficult to understand just what this phenomenon was. But it was real to people in first-century Palestine.

According to Mark's account, the man with the unclean spirit cried out, "What have you to do with us, Jesus of Nazareth? Have you come to destroy us? I know who you are, the Holy One of God" (Mark 1:24).

Jesus rebuked the evil spirit in this troubled man saying: "Be silent, and come out of him!" The result was that "the unclean spirit, convulsing him and crying with a loud voice, came out of him" (Mark 1:25-26). Some interpreters guess that the man might have been suffering from epilepsy, but we cannot be sure because the usual word for "seizure" is not used here when it speaks of "convulsing him." At any rate, the main thrust of the story is that Jesus had authority over demonic powers.

The reaction of the congregation in the synagogue to this work of exorcism was the same as their response to his earlier teaching, namely: "They were all amazed, and they kept on asking one another, 'What is this? A new teaching — with authority! He commands even the unclean spirits, and they obey him' " (Mark 1:27).

Jesus had authority in his teaching showing that the scribes were shallow and stale in their teaching while his was deep and original, and he also had authority in his healing with real power to counteract the forces of evil. The people had never heard or seen anything like this in their previous experience in the synagogue.

We like to be in control but if we are realistic we know that much in our own personal lives as well as in the larger world in general is out of control. We would prefer an orderly, rational, and moral universe but that is not the way things are.

While riding in my car one day I heard the announcement on the radio of a local theater group planning to do the play, *Lord of the Flies*, based on William Golding's novel of the same name. I remember reading the book several years ago. The story involves a group of English boys who survive an airplane crash in the Pacific Ocean only to be stranded on an uninhabited island.

Golding eloquently describes his story with rich symbolism that applies to all humankind. At first, the boys seem to get along very well but gradually conflict develops. Ralph becomes the leader of the group representing reason and order; however, he is soon opposed by Jack and his followers called "hunters" who are obsessed with killing the pigs that roam wild throughout the island. Ostensibly Jack and his "hunters" are looking for food but in time their aim takes on a more sinister look. Ralph feels the all-important task is to build a fire so that someone seeking them would know where to find them. Jack and his followers are not concerned about this task and constantly pursue their own agenda.

Eventually, the followers of Jack descend into all kinds of evil. They begin worshiping a decaying pig's head surrounded by swarming flies, "Lord of the Flies" that could be translated "Beelzebub" — the prince of decay. As the end draws near Simon is killed and Piggy, the most intellectual of the group, is killed too. Jack and his fanatical gang attired as painted savages, set fire to the brush where Ralph is hiding and drive him on to the beach. Just about the time they are prepared to subdue Ralph a British naval officer appears out of nowhere and rescues Ralph and the other boys who did not join Jack in his ferocious attack. The fire set to drive Ralph out into the open actually alerted the British naval officer and his men to the spot where the boys were on the island. In the end the civilized approach of reason and order represented by Ralph won the day.

This is a chilling picture of how life can spin out of control.

Even in small matters we do not have absolute control.

I once read a letter to "Dear Abby" in the newspaper that went something like this:

> Dear Abby: Last week my sister-in-law had a garage sale, and right out front was displayed the gift my husband and I had given her last Christmas. It had never been used and was sold for less than half of what we paid for it. My husband said it was hers to do whatever she pleased with and that I was stupid and oversensitive to give it a second thought. What do you think? Signed. Hurt.

Abby replied, "Dear Hurt: Your husband is right when he says the gift was hers to do with whatever she pleased."

A true gift does leave the giver exposed. The giver is out of control. His or her defenses are down.

On large matters too, we regularly plan something and it backfires on us. During World War II the Manhattan Project was started to produce an atomic bomb. In places like Chicago; Los Alamos, New Mexico; and Oak Ridge, Tennessee, the work went on at a furious pace in secrecy. Finally, near the end of the war the atomic bomb was just about ready to be deployed. The scientists learned that Germany, now weeks away from defeat, was not making the bomb. They questioned whether they should rush to complete their project. Perhaps it would not be needed to defeat the Japanese. Albert Einstein was asked to write a letter to President Franklin D. Roosevelt, on behalf of the scientists to bring him up to date on their progress. The president never read the letter. It was found in his office after he died on April 12, 1945. The letter was passed on to Harry Truman, Roosevelt's successor in office. A decision was made to drop the atomic bomb, first on Hiroshima on August 6, 1945, and then three days later on Nagasaki. Einstein was at his rented cottage at Saranac Lake in the Adirondacks when he heard the news. All he could say was, "Oh, my God."

A month after the bomb was dropped a group of scientists who were involved in creating the atomic bomb signed a statement urging that a council of nations be created to control atomic weaponry. Einstein wanted even greater restrictions calling for a "supranational" entity rather than an "international" one because this organization would exist *above* its member nations rather than be a mediator among sovereign nations. Most scientists thought his scheme was too idealistic and impractical. What all the scientists agreed upon was something had to be done to control this incredible destructive power that had been unleashed by their hands. The bomb had consequences they had not foreseen.

When the scientists first began to work on the Manhattan Project they envisioned all the possibilities of good that could come from their experiments but by the close of the war they recoiled in horror when they realized the destruction that could come to all humankind. Their discovery could be used for bad as well as good ends.[1]

We all appreciate the tremendous advances of science and technology that have made our lives more enjoyable and more exciting in recent years, but we also know that some of these "advances" can be used with bad intentions as well as with good ones. Ever since scientists have unlocked the mystery of the atom we have been living under the threat of "the bomb." Of course, today we exist under a more terrifying nuclear threat than the original atomic bomb.

Even our "best and brightest" minds cannot keep everything under control; therefore, we cannot expect those of us who are more ordinary people to think that we can have complete control over our lives. We have problems we cannot solve, burdens too heavy to bear, and addictions that enslave us. We have diseases we cannot heal and in the end death that we cannot escape.

We may not be able to describe and explain the demon possession mentioned in our scriptural passage today but we have seen our share of the demonic in our world today and even in our own lives. It is a rough world we live in and Mark in his gospel does not want us to forget it, but he doesn't leave us there. He also has good news to tell us. He declares that there is one who is stronger than the evil we confront. Someone more powerful than evil has entered the world and that someone stands by our side to help us battle against evil.

The King's Speech won an Academy Award as the best motion picture of the year. The film depicted the plight of King George VI who came to the throne as World War II approached. He was shy and had a stammer that made ordinary speaking so difficult let alone having to make formal speeches to thousands of people and radio addresses to millions of people. Over against this stammering king who could barely speak at all was Adolf Hitler, a mesmerizing speaker who could control and incite the largest crowds to support the Nazi regime as it sought to conquer all of Europe.

The heart of the film centers in George's wife Elizabeth who seeks to help her husband. In desperation she goes to visit Lionel Logue, a little-known, self-trained speech therapist, who agrees to help her husband, not knowing at the time that he is the King of England. Elizabeth ultimately convinces her reluctant husband to see this odd character.

Over a period of time Logue in his unorthodox way encourages, or threatens might be a better word, the king to learn to speak clearly. He teaches the king to do endless calisthenics. He even has the king singing and cursing. He does a bit of probing into the king's early life and discovers a bad relation with his father and his older brother who can do no wrong in the eyes of the father. Logue tells the king that he is determined "to help you find your voice." In the end of the story, King George VI does find his voice and rallies the people in a radio broadcast that prepares them to stand against Nazi tyranny.

William H. Willimon in a penetrating article in the *Christian Century* magazine used *The King's Speech* movie as a basis for speaking about the authority of preaching the gospel. He argues that it is extremely difficult to teach seminarians how to preach. He explains:

> King George, head of the British Empire, was terrified by the prospect of being put in front of a microphone. That's nothing compared to going head to head with the average North American congregation with nothing to aid you but three points and a poem. To say something important to a crowd of listeners, to dare to intrude

into other people's souls with words, to tell them the truth that they have been assiduously avoiding — that is not a vocation for the faint of heart. Who would undertake it without external compulsion?[2]

Willimon goes on to say that preaching can't be done "without being summoned." He then cites a personal example:

> Sometimes I'm invited to "just share what's on your heart." Alas, as an ordained spokesperson for the gospel, I'm not free to engage in such self-indulgence. Left to my own devices, I might say what I'm really thinking — but the church could care less about what I'm thinking, The pressing question: "Is there any word from the Lord?" That **is** the pressing question![3]

Recognizing the voice of authority is the key to overcoming the chaos, "the out of control" aspect of so much of our lives. There is only one who speaks with an authoritative voice straight from God, namely Jesus who astounded the synagogue congregation in Capernaum that day and who continues to astound today as he subdues the unruly powers that torment us. Amen.

---

1. Walter Isaacson, *Einstein: His Life and Universe* (New York: Simon & Schuster, 2007), 480-488.
2. William H. Willimon, "Voice Lessons," *Christian Century* (Chicago: February 8, 2011), 10-13.
3. *Ibid.*

Developing a Quiet Center

Kathleen Norris tells of an experiment she tried with elementary school children when she taught art. She told them first they get a chance to make noise and then they will make silence.

"The rules for noise were simple: when I raise my hand, I told them, you make all the noise you can while sitting at your desk, using your mouth, hands, and feet. The kid's eyes would grow wide — and the teacher's as well — so I'd add, the important thing is that when I lower my hand, you have to stop."

Kathleen was surprised the school principals didn't come, but she said the roar only lasted a few seconds and the principals probably thought they were imagining the whole thing.

"The rules for silence were equally simple. Don't hold your breath and make funny faces. I learned to say, as this is how third graders typically imagine silence. Just breathe normally but quietly: the only hard thing is to sit so still that you make no noise at all. We always had to try this more than once. A pencil would roll down someone's desk, or someone would shift in a seat. But in every case but one, over many years, I found that children were able to become so still that silence became a presence in the classroom."[1]

If it would only be this easy to recover silence in the midst of the noise in our larger society, how much better life would be.

Today we have Facebook, Twitter, cell phones, and iPhones, all of which serve useful and valuable services, especially in the time of emergency. But do we have to be "connected" with people all the time? Don't we need to develop a "quiet center" apart from our busy, hectic, and noisy world so that we can lessen our stress and get in touch with our inner life?

Mark in his gospel depicts Jesus as a man of action. His whole gospel focuses not on what Jesus said but more on what he did. In the very first chapter Mark describes Jesus healing people who are suffering, casting out demons, replying to impatient disciples, traveling from town to town, and proclaiming the good news in one synagogue after another. Then right smack in the middle of these sentences loaded with action — our text for today — we find these quiet words: "In the morning, while it was still very dark, he got up and went out to a deserted place, and there he prayed" (Mark 1:35).

Not only on this occasion, but throughout Jesus' brief ministry he took time to go apart to a quiet place, especially before important events he sought communion with God. For example, after his baptism, before he began his ministry he went off into the desert for forty days. Jesus took three of his most trusted disciples to a lonely mountaintop where he was transfigured. After the Last Supper Jesus led his disciples to the Garden of Gethsemane where he prayed alone in quiet while his disciples slept.

Again and again Jesus went away to some solitary place, far from the activity of people. He kept the channels open so that he could experience God's fellowship, guidance, and power. He did not always feel the need to be doing something. He did not always have to be useful.

In the Taoist tradition there is a story about a carpenter and his apprentice and an old tree. A carpenter and his apprentice one day were walking through the forest and they came upon a tall, huge, gnarled, old, beautiful oak tree. The carpenter asked the apprentice, "Do you know why this tree is so tall, so huge, so gnarled, so old, and so beautiful?" The apprentice responded, "No... why?" The carpenter explained, "because it is useless. If it had been useful, it would have been cut down long ago and made into tables and chairs, but because it is useless it could grow so tall and so beautiful that you can sit in its shade and relax."[2]

We all need to take some time away from being useful so that we can grow old freely without being preoccupied with doing something. But how do we go about developing a quiet center?

Jesus gives us clues in this brief description of his own quiet center.

First of all, we need to set aside a certain *time*.

For Jesus, in this instance, it was in the morning. And the early morning hours continue to be a favorite time for his followers to commune with God in prayer as they seek to start the day conscious of God's presence. Other people may find the noon hour a good break in the day's activities for quiet time. Still others prefer the evening after the busy day is over to find quiet time. A lot depends on our temperament, or our work schedule, or our age. There is no one absolute, perfect time. We must all find the time that suits us best.

Arthur Paul Boers, a Mennonite scholar who has found helpful the classical "Morning and Evening Hours of Prayers," writes: These regular prayers keep reminding me that God is present, at work, and reliable. Thus such prayers call me to pay attention and to trust that God is active even when I cannot discern God's activity for a long, long time."[3]

I have always admired the painting by Millet called "The Angelus." He pictures a peasant couple bowing in prayer. They had just heard the Angelus bells ringing from the church bell tower in the village. They have stopped their work in the field. They pause for a moment of silent prayer to reconnect their lives to God. The strain and bitterness leave their souls and their troubles as well and their work is seen in a new light.

Through the years I have loved the sound of bells. They remind me to cease what I am doing and for a moment center my thoughts. When I hear our church bell ring five minutes before worship it reminds me it is stop time, it is "catch my breath" time; it is time to be grateful to God; it is time to restore the rhythm of life between work and rest.

Then there is the matter of *place*. Where is the best place for a quiet center? For Jesus it was a "deserted place" apart from the crowds. On occasion that "deserted place" was in a garden, on a mountaintop, or in the desert itself.

What works for me is sitting in my favorite chair early each morning before the day's work begins. This practice enables me to center down and reminds me to be attentive to God. Some days the quiet time consists of fifteen minutes, other times it is longer or shorter. But I know it if I do not spend this time alone. I might add that this is not a time for planning the day's schedule. I have a tendency of doing too much planning and I have to constantly check myself. No, this not a time to plan anything but simply to listen to what God might have to say to me.

What about *method* in developing our quiet center? Jesus does not say very much about method or methods. We do not know exactly how he prayed and made contact with God. His followers have used a variety of methods in order to keep in contact with God.

There is no one method that is the only method as Teresa A. Blythe suggests from the title of her recent book, *50 Ways to Pray*. Blythe says: "Like many Protestant Christians, I grew up thinking there was only one way to pray… It wasn't until I met a spiritual director in the late 1980s that I was invited to pray in new and different ways."[4]

Some Christians rely heavily on silence. Just being alone with God in the silence without any elaborate form of prayer to follow is enough for many people.

Chaim Potok in his fascinating novel, *The Chosen*, tells the story of two Jewish boys from totally different backgrounds who come together because of their common love of baseball. The one boy is from the strict Hasidic home of a rabbi where silence, meditation, and prayer are taken for granted. The other boy is from a family of Reform Jews who are liberal, rational, and sophisticated. The Hasidic boy tries to explain what silence means to him: "You can listen to silence, Reuven. I've begun to realize that you listen to silence and learn from it. It has a quality and a dimension all its own. It talks to me sometimes. I feel myself alive in it. It talks. I can hear it."[5]

Could we have such an experience? We could experiment a few minutes each day in a solitary place, centering down, and listening to God. If we did that, we might never be the same.

I know it is not easy to do. No sooner do we attempt to be silent then countless distractions appear. When will I have time to prepare the meal? We worry about our next doctor's appointment. We think of all the work that is left unfinished.

In order to counteract these distractions a variety of techniques have been developed. We might pay attention to our breathing. Inhale slowly. Then exhale. Breathe in good thoughts; exhale bad thoughts. Another way to center down is to repeat a word or phrase over and over again as we descend into the silence. For some people any word will do as a mantra, but for Christians a verse of scripture seems more appropriate, for example, "Be still, and know that I am God..." (Psalm 46:10).

Another way of combating distractions while attempting to remain in the silence is to incorporate the distraction into the silence itself, make it a part of your prayer to God.

Another method that may be used in developing a quiet center is to pray for others, to engage in intercessory prayer. Scientists constantly remind us today in our "post-modern" age that the universe is "interconnected." We are surrounded by fields of invisible energy. Likewise, in human relationships no one lives alone, but we are caught up in a spider's web of connections. We can and do influence each other. Although intercessory prayer remains a mystery in just how it works, we know that Jesus set the example in praying for others, and the apostle Paul reminds us that even today the Spirit prays through us "with sighs too deep for words" (Romans 8:26). When we pray for others we are only adding to the cosmic love of God who cares. Healing takes place in intercessory prayer — it may be physical healing, or emotional healing, or spiritual healing. It is not always physical healing but God's healing presence is exhibited in some way when we pray for others.

In fourteenth-century England it was not uncommon for a small group of women to settle in a room at the base of some church and give themselves to intercessory prayer on behalf of the church and its members. They were called "anchorites." Indeed, they were anchors who held the church together amidst the storms and struggles of their day.

We too need "anchorites" in our own time, men and women, young and old, active and homebound — who are willing to pray passionately for our own congregation. What higher calling could we have than to be used to channel God's loving power to others?

The methods used in a quiet center are numerous today, but one other one should be mentioned. It goes by an ancient Latin title, *Lectio Divina*, which plainly means "spiritual reading" or "sacred reading." This approach uses prayer and the Bible, in fact it consists of four main elements: *lectio* (reading), *mediatio* (meditation), *oratio* (prayer), and *contemplatio* (contemplation).

We begin with reading. We choose some portion of scripture and begin with a time of silence. We open our hearts to God to see what God has to say to us. God's word is first and then we respond to the word. It is helpful to read the scripture passage aloud. Also, reading is best done if the scripture selection is not too long, just a few verses will do.

Next we engage in meditation. We linger over the text. We might concentrate on only part of the scriptures assigned, possible only a verse, or a phrase, or even a word. We can take as much time as we need. We can be like a cow chewing his cud. All too often we read the scriptures quickly without letting the words sink deeply into our very being. In a word, we ruminate over the text, perhaps repeating it again and again like a mantra.

We then proceed to prayer. We open our hearts to God and articulate our deepest feelings in the light of the word of the scriptures that we are wrestling with in our innermost being. Our prayers interact with God's word. We express how this word that we have been meditating upon connects with our own life in some specific way. If we are having difficulty in expressing ourselves in prayer, we can find no better resource than the book of Psalms to guide us. The Psalms speak to us of every human emotion. The Psalms provide us with the words to respond to God's word, and even more importantly, they confront us with the real world and not a dream world in which we would like to live.

Finally, we come to contemplation. There is much misunderstanding over this word. We may conjure up monks and nuns who live apart from normal everyday living praying all the time. We who have responsibilities of family life and go to the workplace daily do not have this luxury, valuable as the work the monastic orders do provide for us all.

Contemplation as it is usually is understood in *Lectio Divina* is something far more practical. After we have read, meditated, and prayed, we contemplate all that we have done to the totality of our lives. We do this, however, with a newly gained consciousness of God with us in all that we do. In other words, to contemplate does not mean retreating from the world; on the contrary it means living what we have just read, meditated upon, and prayed. We might add that contemplation is not just for a select few but for everyone seeking to develop a quiet center. One of the best definitions I have heard of contemplation is "Contemplation means living what we read, not wasting any of it or hoarding any of it, but using it up in living."[6]

I know of one group who calls themselves the C.I.A., "Contemplatives in Action," not a bad name for those people who have captured the essential meaning of contemplation.

Robert Russell, once a professor of English at Franklin & Marshall College in Lancaster, Pennsylvania, in his autobiography titled *To Catch an Angel*, tells of his love of fishing along the St. Lawrence River. He had a cottage on one of the Thousand Islands. The fact that he is blind complicates his fishing. He explains how he does it:

> So that I can go out by myself, whenever I please, I have run a wire down to the end of the dock, where I have mounted a large electric bell. Before I go down to the dock, I plug the line into an outlet in the house. A timing device permits the bell to ring once every thirty seconds. If I row too far upwind to be able to hear the bell, I can still fish without anxiety because I can drift downwind and then I am again in touch with my base.

Russell goes on to add:

And a man needs a base to quest from and needs the sense that, however, far he has strayed, return is still possible.... The river lies before me, a constant invitation, a constant challenge, and my bell is the thread of sound along which I return. To a quiet base.[7]

We all are in a way like that blind man on the river. God has called us on a journey, out on the river, to go with the flow, but not to forget our quiet base and to return to it often to reset our bearings before continuing again.

The way to silence our noisy hearts in the hectic environment in which we live today is developing a quiet center. Amen.

---

1. Kathleen Norris, *Amazing Grace: A Vocabulary of Faith* (New York: Riverhead Book, a member of Penguin Putnam Inc., 1998), 16-17.

2. Henri J.M. Nouwen, *Out of Solitude* (Notre Dame, Indiana: Ave Maria Press, 1974), 22-23.

3. Arthur Paul Boers, *The Rhythm of God's Grace* (Brewster, Massachusetts: Paraclete Press, 2003), xix.

4. Teresa A. Blythe, *50 Ways to Pray: Practices from Many Traditions and Times* (Nashville: Abingdon Press, 2006), 11.

5. Chaim Potok, *The Chosen* (New York: Fawcett Crest, published by Ballatine Books, 1967), 249.

6. Eugene H. Peterson, *Eat This Book: A Conversation in the Art of Spiritual Reading* (Grand Rapids: William B. Eerdmans Publishing Company, 2006), 113.

7. Robert Russell, *To Catch an Angel* (New York: The Vanguard Press, Inc., 1962), 313-314.

Daring to Touch

Sam Keen in his book, *To a Dancing God*, tells of accidentally tripping over a rock one day while working at his summer farm in Maine. He began talking to the rock and the rock talked back. The dialogue went something like this:

Keen: "... Why did you trip me?"

Rock: "I didn't trip you. I'm just lying here in my space conversing with the sky and the ground and you come up and kick me."

Keen: "Well, never mind that. I see now that you are just about the right shape and size for a wall I am building."

Rock: "First you accuse me of abusing you, but now it is clear that you are the aggressor who is lacking in regard for me. You still haven't seen me. All you can see is a use to which I may be put. Why don't you exercise your facility of wonder for a moment?"

Keen: "I suppose I could try. What would you like me to do?"

Rock: "Look at the nuances of color in me for a beginning. Then you might notice the gracefulness of my form (far too fine to be hidden in a wall). Finally, if you can muster sufficient imagination, run your hands fondly over me and feel my massed energy and at least ask yourself the fantastic question of what my reality is like from the inside. Well — what do you think? You seem rather silent."

Keen: "When I take the time to look at you from different perspectives to welcome your strangeness into my consciousness I am both rewarded and confused. I see your beauty now and not merely your usefulness.

But I still have a wall to build. Any suggestions?"
Rock: "No, I don't know how you can solve your dilemma of both reverencing and utilizing, but I know that once you have welcomed me into your awareness you will not be so simple-minded as to suppose rocks and trees exist only to trip you or as raw materials for construction of walls and houses. Next time you come this way you might even look to keep from disturbing my rest."[1]

Admittedly, not all rocks talk like that, but occasionally you will stumble over a "philosophical" rock that will answer back.

If rocks respond in such a manner, how much more do human beings feel slighted and misused when we do not recognize their intrinsic worth or see them only in a utilitarian way — how we use them to satisfy our own selfish ends. Are we aware of others? Do we see them? Do we touch them? Does our life really touch others around us in a significant way?

Of course, we should say at the outset that not all touching is good. We cannot touch fire without getting hurt. There also is insincere touching. We cannot violate sacred human relationships of other people by touching them inappropriately. We have all read enough about child abuse and spousal abuse to know what we mean. We can abuse our capacity to touch but by and large life is made for touching.

The next significant encounter Mark mentions in Jesus' movement around Galilee is with a leper who comes to him, kneels down, and begs him, "If you choose, you can make me clean" (Mark 1:40).

The leper was an outcast in society. We are not certain about the details of this man's condition. By Jesus' time all kinds of skin diseases were often grouped together under the heading of leprosy. Whatever the specifics might be such a skin disease rendered the person unclean in the presence of others. A person in this condition was separated from society and when he did appear he had to warn others to get out of the way. He was shunned from the rest of human contact.

The leper's words show an element of trust in Jesus even though the words may not represent a full knowledge of faith in Jesus as the Messiah. At least the leper believed that Jesus could heal him.

Jesus' response is worth noting too. Mark records, "Moved with pity, Jesus stretched out his hand and touched him, and said to him, 'I do choose. Be made clean!' " Jesus' compassion reached out to this unfortunate human being not only with words but he "touched him" — he touched the untouchable.

Some New Testament scholars have pointed out that some Greek manuscripts, not the earliest ones, read that Jesus was moved with "anger" not "pity." If "anger" is the proper translation then according to Lamar Williamson Jr., it might mean: "The healing of the leper is then an example of Jesus' aggressive action against all that is unclean and destructive."[2]

Most interpreters of this passage agree that "pity" or "compassion" is the more accurate meaning of Jesus' words, and it certainly harmonizes with the totality of Jesus' healing ministry.

After Jesus spoke the affirming words to the leper, we have one of Mark's favorite words "immediately." "Immediately the leprosy left him, and he was made clean" (Mark 1:42). Then we have Jesus' stern orders that he tell no one else about what has happened but go directly to the priest for the ceremonial ritual of cleansing. In so doing, the man made well by Jesus could now re-enter society. The book of Leviticus, chapters 13-14, in the Hebrew Bible spells out the details of this ritual.

Mark often has Jesus saying after a miracle has occurred that the person or persons involved should not spread the word around. Many people are mystified by this command. In the gospel of Mark Jesus is portrayed as the "Hidden Messiah." Why? Could it be with so many erroneous views of the Messiah floating around at this time that Jesus did not want to confuse the masses who came to hear him? He was waiting for the opportune time to declare that he was the Messiah. The time was not now.

Nonetheless, the healed leper did the opposite of what Jesus told him to do, and he went out and told everyone what had happened. The result was that Jesus could no longer enter towns because of the crowds. He was forced to stay in the countryside. Even there people flocked to find him.

It should be noted in passing that Jesus never used his healing to call attention to himself. His teaching and healing ministry were done to call attention to the fact that the kingdom of God had arrived.

Those who saw these signs were invited to enter the kingdom.

Jesus has demonstrated for us the tremendous power of touch. Many doctors and nurses have been inspired to enter the medical profession exhibiting similar compassion in treating patients, even sometimes at the risk of their own lives. For all of us, the call is not to be afraid of the "untouchables" in our own day (the outcasts whoever they may be). If we are Jesus' disciples we too will reach out and identify and seek to rectify the wrongs being done to so many people in our present society.

Sociologist James B. Stockinger shares this reflection on touch:

> Each of us lives in and through an immense movement of the hands of other people. The hands of other people grow the food we eat, weave the clothes we wear, and build the shelters we inhabit. The hands of other people give pleasure to our bodies in moments of passion and aid and comfort in times of affliction and

distress. It is in and through the hands of other people that the commonwealth of nature is appropriated and accommodated to the needs and pleasures of our separate individual lives, and, at the end, it is the hands of other people that lower us into the earth.[3]

In a sense, we receive ourselves as a gift from the hands of others.

I heard of a young man who decided he wanted to learn how to better relate to others. He went into a bookstore and at first was hard pressed to find anything to help him. Finally, he came upon a book that seemed to be helpful. It was titled, *How to Hug*. When he returned home, unfortunately, he found that he had bought Volume 9 of an encyclopedia.

There is good reading around today to help us to express ourselves more intimately with others. Life indeed is made for touching. Robert Corin Morris tells of an exercise he has used with lay pastoral calling groups. He calls it "the deepening touch," and he explains:

First, we practiced reaching out and taking a person's hand in an ordinary, casual way holding it for a half-minute. Then we practiced "deepening" the touch. People were directed to take a few moments to feel the aliveness in their own hand, and to awaken a sense of intentional caring. Then, with "awakened" hearts and hands, they reached out to hold the other person's hand.[4]

The difference that was made by conscious awareness and intention surprised the group members and they felt more "connected" to the other person and even felt that God was in their midst.

I believe people come to worship today because they want an encounter with Jesus. They want to be touched by him, to really experience him. They want to be changed and transformed by him, even as the leper was in Mark's story.

As we all know, numerous churches are celebrating Holy Communion more often than before. As we participate in the Eucharist we not only hear the word of God proclaimed, but we have the opportunity to touch and handle "things unseen" as the hymn writer puts it.

In our particular congregation every board and committee meeting ends with the group holding hands and repeating the Mizpah benediction: "The Lord watch between you and me when we are absent one from the another." It is the touch of genuine fellowship. Also, not a few churches close their worship services with all the people holding hands and saying an appropriate prayer or singing a fitting song.

Recently, I had the privilege and great joy of attending an ordination service of a close friend. One of the high points in the service for me was when it came time for the ordination itself and the laying on of hands with prayer. Ministers of the word in the congregation as well as those ministers who led the service were called up to participate in the laying on of hands. This was a singular moment for me because I had worked closely with the young man to be ordained from the very beginning when we first sensed God might be calling him to prepare for Christian ministry. We all touched him praying that the Holy Spirit would indeed empower him to preach the word, administer the sacraments, and exercise the responsibilities of pastor and teacher.

What followed also involved touching as not only the senior pastor and the mother of the newly ordained minister but practically everyone present enthusiastically and joyfully hugged the young man. It was a happy celebration from beginning to end!

When I was a young boy I was playing touch football out in the street in front of my house one relatively warm December Sunday afternoon. Our play suddenly was interrupted by someone shouting out the door, "The Japanese have bombed Pearl Harbor!"

Most of us didn't know very much about Pearl Harbor. We soon learned it was in Hawaii in the Pacific Ocean, a territory of the United States. We became aware of the fact that almost the entire American naval fleet had been destroyed that day. Soon we were at war. World War II had begun for America, even as it had begun earlier for our soon-to-become Allies in Europe.

Since that time I have read a great deal about Pearl Harbor and World War II, and I have seen numerous movies about the day President Franklin D. Roosevelt said would live in infamy. I thought I had a pretty good grasp of what happened at that time, but it wasn't until a few years ago when my wife and I visited Pearl Harbor while vacationing in Hawaii that I really sensed it in a more visceral way.

Daily more than 4,000 people stand in line waiting to be taken in a small group by a craft that slowly makes its way out to the Pearl Harbor Memorial in the harbor. Few people speak during the trip. When you arrive at the Memorial itself and begin to walk from one end to the other, you notice at the center the floor dips. You can feel it and you come to understand that this sensation marks the low point in World War II and then the floor rises at the end to symbolize the ultimate victory in the war.

The Memorial is a 184-foot concrete structure that straddles the midsection of the *USS Arizona* where most of the 1,177 crewmen who died aboard the ship that fateful day are still entombed. As you look down at the sunken ship with some turrets protruding from the water you have an eerie feeling. When you come to the far end of the Memorial a white marble wall contains the names of the victims of this tragedy. You can reach up and touch the name of your loved one, if you wish. No one can spend even a little time at this Memorial without being profoundly touched.

We might add that the Vietnam Memorial in Washington DC designed by the Yale University student Maya Ying Lin has had a similar effect upon all who have visited it. At first, many veteran groups criticized the memorial, but in time as more and more Vietnam veterans came to pay their respects to see the names of their comrades and touch their names, they were emotionally moved in a way they never expected. Today the memorial has become America's version of the "wailing wall." This memorial probably has done more to heal the oozing wounds of the Vietnam War than any other single thing.

Jesus touched people and made them whole. We too can bring healing by our touch. When we offer a warm handshake, or give someone a hug, we express our concern in a way that words can never do. There are many lonely and hurting people all around us who yearn for a loving touch. Let us look for an opening to meet their deepest needs. Amen.

---

1. Sam Keen, *To a Dancing God* (New York: Harper & Row, 1970), 28-29.

2. Lamar Williamson Jr., *Interpretation: A Bible Commentary for Teaching and Preaching* (Louisville: John Knox Press, 1983), 59.

3. James B. Stockinger, University of California Ph.D. dissertation, "Locke and Rousseau: Human Nature, Human Citizenship and Human Work," as printed in Robert Neely Bellah, et al., *The Good Society* (New York: Alfred A. Knopf, 1991), 104.

4. Robert Corin Morris, *Wrestling with Grace: A Spirituality for the Rough Edges of Daily Life* (Nashville: Upper Room Books, 2003), 49.

Facing the
Future with Hope

A euphemism according to the dictionary is the "substitution of an agreeable expression for something that may be unpleasant."

One of the best explanations of this word that I know was given by former Senator Everett Dirkson from Illinois. He called a euphemism "something that seems what it ain't." He went on to tell a story to illustrate the foolishness of euphemisms.

He said, "I am reminded of the man who filled in an application for an insurance policy. One of the questions he had to answer was 'How old was your father when he died and of what did he die?'

"Well, his father had been hanged for a crime he had committed, but he did not want to put that on his application. He puzzled over it quite a while. Finally, he wrote: 'My father was 65 when he died. He came to his end while participating in a public function when the platform gave way.' "

That's one way to put it. That's a euphemism — trying to say something unpleasant in an agreeable way.

Peter had a tendency to speak in euphemisms. He confessed that Jesus was the Messiah, but he didn't like the notion Jesus added that the Messiah was going to suffer and die at the hands of his enemies. Peter could not accept that view; therefore, he held on to his belief that nothing unpleasant must happen to the Messiah.

In commenting upon the transfiguration in Mark 9:1-9, New Testament scholar Lamar Williamson Jr. says, "Here is pure transcendence, of a sort found nowhere else in Mark."[1] Jesus had taken his inner circle of trusted disciples — Peter, James, and John — to a remote retreat high in the mountains, probably Mount Hermon, more than 9,000 feet high, north of Galilee. This setting is not too far away from Caesarea Philippi where Peter had recently made his great confession of faith that Jesus was the Messiah, the Son of God. The high mountain was frequently thought of as the place nearest to heaven. The cloud symbolized for the Hebrew people the presence of God.

What happened in Jesus' transfiguration on the mount? Mark describes this vision or theophany in the following way:

> And he was transfigured before them, and his clothes became dazzling white, such as no one on earth could bleach them. And there appeared to them Elijah with Moses, who were talking with Jesus.
>
> — Mark 9:2-4

The dazzling white clothes of Jesus would remind the faithful Jews of the Shekinah glory and the pillar of fire that led ancient Israel through the wilderness on their way to the Promised Land. Elijah representing the prophets and Moses representing the Law also had life-changing episodes on the mountaintop of Sinai.

Peter, overwhelmed by everything, suggested that they remain on the mountain and build three dwellings, one for Jesus, one for Moses, and one for Elijah. Once again a cloud appeared and a voice spoke out of the cloud saying, "This is my Son, the Beloved; listen to him!" (Mark 9:7). These were the same words that God spoke to Jesus at his baptism. Peter in his call for three dwellings might have had in mind a connection with the Feast of Booths that celebrated God's providence toward his people in that same trek through the desert mentioned above. We cannot be certain of Peter's motivation at this point. Nevertheless, when Peter, James, and John looked around after the cloud passed by, "They saw no one with them any more, but only Jesus" (Mark 9:8).

Although Peter was confused and disheartened by the rebuke Jesus had given him regarding his "soft" view of the Messiah, the transfiguration scene and God's confirmation of Jesus as his Son should have given him confidence to believe good would emerge from Jesus' suffering and death. As they were descending the mountain, Jesus ordered them not to tell anyone about this incident "until after the Son of Man had risen from the dead." In other words, the transfiguration was a preview of something even greater, namely, the resurrection. God's raising Jesus from the dead would become their greatest motivation of all in facing the future with hope.

Therefore, we can say for our present time hope exists for each individual, the church, society, and even the bereaved.

There is hope that each individual might realize his or her potential by the grace of God.

The Rookie tells the true story of Jim Morris who suffered a number of injuries in his professional baseball career and decided his family needed him to work in some other capacity. As an avocation he coached the local high school baseball team, a team that tended to lose more games than they won. One day some of his players saw him warming up and tossing 95-mile-an-hour fastballs. Despite their losing season, Morris challenged his players not to quit but to dream of doing better things in the future. The players talked among themselves and then presented the coach with a challenge of their own. They wanted him to take his own advice. The deal they struck with him was if they turned around their losing ways and finished the season with a championship, then he should agree to try out again to play professional baseball.

The players had seen the gift that Jim had and they wanted him to use it. They said to him, "It's funny that you can't see it, but we can."

As it happened his high school team did win their championship and amidst their celebration they reminded the coach, "Now, it's your turn." Jim Morris did try out for a minor league team and made the team. Later, he was called up to the major leagues where he pitched effectively for two years. His family and the whole town rallied around him and went to see his major league debut with much pride in their hearts.

What do we see? Can we see the gift someone has and that person does not even know it exists? Has God given us the gift of insight or observation that needs to be shared with others? Has something happened in our own brokenness that is worth sharing with others who may have similar struggles? Are we learning a new way of "seeing," not what everybody says is there, but what God is showing us through the "eyes of faith"?

There is hope for the church today, even though many people are pessimistic about its future.

Once, when I was meeting with church leaders in doing long-range planning, I had them sit in a circle in the form of a clock. With the oldest member at 1:00 o'clock we went around clockwise until at 11:00 o'clock we sat the newest member. Then I asked the same question to each one present, "Who was the person you remember when you first united with the church? Who was the key leader and perhaps someone who helped you in those early years?" What spellbinding stories we heard of strong men and women of faith who made a difference in the lives of the congregation at that time and in the life of the one who was telling the story. Since then I have become convinced that God calls people of faith in every generation to move the church forward. There is never a time when a vibrant witness is not being made.

Douglas Steere recalls what happened to the College of William and Mary in Virginia during the Civil War. The college was closed because all the students were fighting in the war. Many accepted the college's future as doomed but an old custodian refused to accept this verdict. Steere said: "Each day for five years he rang the bells of this ghost college as though it still lived. At the end of the five years, he rang them for a reopening that vindicated his vigil of faith."[2]

There is hope for the wider society too.

We might not think that the New Testament scholar and prolific author N.T. Wright would have a keen interest in current social justice issues, but he does. He is principally concerned about the massive economic imbalance of the world whose major symptom is the ridiculous and unpayable Third World debt. He argues: "The present system of global debt is the real immoral scandal, the dirty little secret — or rather the enormous secret — of glitzy, glossy Western capitalism. Whatever it takes, we must change this situation or stand condemned by subsequent history alongside those who supported slavery two centuries ago and those who supported the Nazi seventy years ago. It is that serious."

We can be grateful for men and women like N.T. Wright who focus on a particular social justice issue and then do everything they can to help alleviate the burden of the people affected by the injustice.

Finally, there is hope for the bereaved.

Nothing is as traumatic as to lose a loved one unless it is to lose two loved ones at the same time. Michael Yaconelli tells of a friend who had waited with his wife a long time before they could have children. At last the day arrived when the man's wife became pregnant. Within a few months they even had better news and learned that she was to have twins. How happy the couple felt but then the unraveling began. During a routine checkup the doctor discovered that one of the babies had already died and the other had little chance of surviving.

Yaconelli invited his friend to attend a retreat with him thinking such an experience would be helpful to him in his grief. His friend attended reluctantly. He did not want to be around people. One of the exercises during the retreat was to take a nature walk. The spiritual director instructed everyone to look for signs of God in the natural world. His friend was furious, and he exclaimed: "This is stupid. As far as I am concerned, God is not anywhere. I am not going to waste an hour trying to find God in nature."

He went away from the rest of the men and sought to sabotage the experiment by finding a long stairway of cement where he would walk, gazing only at the cement and not at the beauty that surrounded him. Later, he came back and told the group what had happened to him. "I was about halfway up the walkway, walking very slowly, lost in my anger and resentment toward God, when the tears began. I was not conscious of my tears until my mind caught up with my heart. There were cracks in the cement. The entire walkway was covered with cracks; they were caused by what was in the cracks — in every crack, a flower! Somehow, in the midst of the gray lifeless cement, *life made its way through* the impenetrable rock and mortar of the sidewalk! Suddenly I was conscious of God. He was alive! He surprised me with flowers. He found a way to show me hope in the midst of my despair...."[3]

In closing, I share a story I heard about a salesman from the north eating his first meal in South Carolina. Famished he stopped by a roadside diner and ordered a breakfast of scrambled eggs and sausage. He was taken by surprise, however, when his order came back and there was a white glob of something on his plate. "What's that?" he asked the waitress. "That's grits, sir" she replied. "But I didn't order them," he said. "Honey, you don't order grits," she responded, "They just come."

That's something like the amazing grace of God. You don't order it. It just comes in the most surprising places and at the most unexpected times. My wish for you all is that in the days ahead you will have a heaping plate of grits, namely, numerous serendipity adventures of God breaking into your lives again and again emboldening you to face the future with hope. Amen.

---

1. Lamar Williamson Jr., *Interpretation: A Bible Commentary for Teaching and Preaching:* (Louisville: John Knox Press, 1983), 158.
2. Douglas V. Steere, *Dimensions of Prayer: Cultivating a Relationship with God* (Nashville: Upper Room Books, 1997), 90.
3. Michael Yaconelli, *Messy Sprituality: God's Annoying Love for Imperfect People* (Grand Rapids: Zondervan, 2002), 130-132.

www.ingramcontent.com/pod-product-compliance
Lightning Source LLC
LaVergne TN
LVHW051648080426
835511LV00016B/2562